P9-BYC-229

THE new biology

CANCER

The Role of Genes, Lifestyle, and Environment

Joseph Panno, Ph.D.

Facts On File, Inc.

For my wife, Diana,
who worked with me in the lab for many years,
and for my daughter Eleanor,
who knew about cells before she could read or write.

CANCER: The Role of Genes, Lifestyle, and Environment

Facts On File, Inc.
132 West 31st Street
New York NY 10001

Library of Congress Cataloging-in-Publication Data

Panno, Joseph.
Cancer : the role of genes, lifestyle, and environment / Joseph Panno.
p. cm. — (The "new biology" series)
Includes bibliographical references and index.
ISBN 0-8160-4950-5
1. Cancer—Social aspects. 2. Cancer—Environmental aspects. 3. Cancer—Genetic aspects. I. Title.
RC262.P35 2004
616.99'4071—dc22 2003025840

Facts On File books are available at special discounts when purchased in bulk quantities for businesses, associations, institutions, or sales promotions. Please call our Special Sales Department in New York at (212) 967-8800 or (800) 322-8755.

You can find Facts On File on the World Wide Web at http://www.factsonfile.com

Text design by Erika K. Arroyo
Cover design by Pehrsson Design
Illustrations by Richard Garratt and Joseph Panno

Printed in the United States of America

MP FOF 10 9 8 7 6 5 4 3 2 1

This book is printed on acid-free paper.

CONTENTS

Preface		vii
Acknowledgments		ix
Introduction		xi
1	***Common Types of Cancer***	***1***
	Terminology	2
	Bladder Cancer	4
	Brain Tumors	5
	Breast Cancer	8
	Leukemia	10
	Lung Cancer	12
	Prostate Cancer	14
	Skin Cancer	16
2	***Cancer Cells***	***19***
	Cancer Cells Are Immortal	19
	Broken Chromosomes	21
	A Failure to Communicate	23
	They Go Where They Please	24
	One Mutation Is Not Enough	25
3	***The Road to Oncogenesis***	***27***
	Cancer and the Cell Cycle	28
	A Disease of the Genes	30
	Tumor Suppressor Genes	31
	Oncogenes and Proto-oncogenes	32
	A Dangerous Mix	34

4 *Cancer Progression* 35
Cancers Develop from a Single Bad Cell 35
The Switch from Benign to Malignant Tumors 36
The Role of Sex Hormones 36
Aging and the Incidence of Cancer 37
Carcinogens 38

5 *Cancer Therapies* 42
Angiogenesis Blockers 42
Biotherapies 44
Bone Marrow Transplants 46
Chemotherapy 47
Cryosurgery 50
Gene Therapy 50
Laser Therapy 51
Photodynamic Therapy 52
Radiotherapy 53
Stem Cell Therapy 54

6 *Cancer Around the World* 55
The Magnitude of the Problem 55
Developed Countries Have the Highest Cancer Rates 57
Cancer and the North American Diet 59
Cancer and Lifestyle 62
Cancer and the Environment 65
Summary 65

7 *Clinical Trials* 67
The Four Phases 67
Breast Cancer 69
Chemotherapy 71
Colon Cancer 72
Lung Cancer 72

Melanoma 73
Metastasis 74

8 *Resource Center* 76
Eukaryote Cell Primer 76
Recombinant DNA Primer 96
Gene Therapy Primer 107
Matching Tissues 111
The Human Genome Project 115

Glossary 119
Further Reading 145
Index 151

PREFACE

The New Biology set consists of the following six volumes: *The Cell, Animal Cloning, Stem Cell Research, Gene Therapy, Cancer,* and *Aging.* The set is intended primarily for middle and high school students, but it is also appropriate for first-year university students and the general public. In writing this set, I have tried to balance the need for a comprehensive presentation of the material, covering many complex fields, against the danger of burying—and thereby losing—young students under a mountain of detail. Thus the use of lengthy discussions and professional jargon has been kept to a minimum, and every attempt has been made to ensure that this be done without sacrificing the important elements of each topic. A large number of drawings are provided throughout the series to illustrate the subject matter.

The term *new biology* was coined in the 1970s with the introduction of recombinant DNA technology (or biotechnology). At that time, biology was largely a descriptive science in danger of going adrift. Microbiologists at the turn of the century had found cures for a few diseases, and biologists in the 1960s had cracked the genetic code, but there was still no way to study the function of a gene or the cell as a whole. Biotechnology changed all that, and scientists of the period referred to it as the new technique or the new biology. However, since that time it has become clear that the advent of biotechnology was only the first step toward a new biology, a biology that now includes nuclear transfer technology (animal cloning), gene therapy, and stem cell therapy. All these technologies are covered in the six volumes of this set.

The cell is at the very heart of the new biology and thus figures prominently in this book series. Biotechnology was specifically designed for studying cells, and using those techniques, scientists gained insights into cell structure and function that came with unprecedented detail. As knowledge of the cell grew, the second wave of technologies—animal cloning, stem cell therapy, and gene therapy—began to appear throughout the 1980s and 1990s. The technologies and therapies of the new biology are now being used to treat a wide variety of medical disorders, and someday they may be used to repair a damaged heart, a severed spinal cord, and perhaps even reverse the aging process. These procedures are also being used to enhance food crops and the physical characteristics of dairy cows and to create genetically modified sheep that produce important pharmaceuticals. The last application alone could save millions of lives every year.

While the technologies of the new biology have produced some wonderful results, some of the procedures are very controversial. The ability to clone an animal or genetically engineer a plant raises a host of ethical questions and environmental concerns. Is a cloned animal a freak that we are creating for our entertainment, or is there a valid medical reason for producing such animals? Should we clone ourselves, or use the technology to re-create a loved one? Is the use of human embryonic stem cells to save a patient dying from leukemia a form of high-tech cannibalism? These and many other questions are discussed throughout the series.

The New Biology set is laid out in a specific order, indicated previously, that reflects the natural progression of the discipline. That is, knowledge of the cell came first, followed by animal cloning, stem cell therapy, and gene therapy. These technologies were then used to expand our knowledge of, and develop therapies for, cancer and aging. Although it is recommended that *The Cell* be read first, this is not essential. Volumes 2 through 6 contain extensive background material, located in the final chapter, on the cell and other new biology topics. Consequently, the reader may read the set in the order he or she prefers.

ACKNOWLEDGMENTS

I would first like to thank my friend and mentor, the late Dr. Karun Nair, for helping me understand some of the intricacies of the biological world and for encouraging me to seek that knowledge by looking beyond the narrow confines of any one discipline. The clarity and accuracy of the initial manuscript for this book was greatly improved by reviews and comments from Diana Dowsley and Michael Panno, and later by Frank Darmstadt, Executive Editor; Dorothy Cummings, Project Editor; and Anthony Sacramone, Copy Editor. I am also indebted to Ray Spangenburg, Kit Moser, Sharon O'Brien, and Diana Dowsley for their help in locating photographs for the New Biology set. Finally, I would like to thank my wife and daughter, to whom this book is dedicated, for the support and encouragement that all writers need and are eternally grateful for.

INTRODUCTION

Cancers are produced by cells that have gone mad. Normal cells, on the other hand, are the sanest things in the world. They are polite and enjoy the company of other cells. As a community, they work together for the good of the many, are well organized, hardworking, and content with their lot in life. Heart cells enjoy pumping blood, brain cells would not change places with skin cells for anything under the Sun, and no way would any of them do anything that would jeopardize the health of the body they so carefully constructed. Cancer cells do not care about any of this. They do what they want and go where they please. If they decide to build a large tumor in the middle of the brain, well, that is what they are going to do, even if it kills the body they are living in.

Taming a cancer cell is hard to do and usually fails. Normally, surgeons just cut them out or try to kill them in some way. It is a brutal game from start to finish. But advances in the past 10 years are making it possible to deal with this disease in a more elegant fashion. Scientists know now that a cancer cell's madness is a fever of the genes, a fever that destroys the cell's communication network and its ability to control its own reproduction. Many of the affected genes have been identified, and by restoring them to health we can stop the cancer.

Although cancers have been diagnosed for the past 100 years, physicians were at a loss to explain the underlying causes of the disease. Throughout much of the 1900s, scientists believed that cancer was caused by a microbial infection. Indeed, certain tumors found in chickens, known as sarcomas, were shown to be infected with a virus, but most human cancers showed no such infection. Consequently, the cause of this disease remained a mystery for many years even after the introduction of recombinant DNA technology in the 1970s. Many investigators at that time believed the cell's genes were the main culprit, but there seemed to be no way to identify those genes or even to estimate the number of genes that might be involved.

The breakthrough came in the 1980s when scientists began reexamining the chicken sarcoma and, in particular, the virus that was always associated with this cancer. Using recombinant DNA technology, scientists showed that one of the virus's genes was responsible for inducing the cancer. The identification of this gene, called *src* (pronounced "sark"), provided a direct link between a gene and cancer induction. The identification of a cancer-causing gene (now known as an oncogene) was extremely important but it did not address the fact that most cancers are not associated with a viral infection. The resolution to this puzzle came when investigators searched the chicken genome for a gene similar to *src*. To their great surprise, they not only found *src* but they were able to show that this gene originated in the chicken genome and was picked up by the virus during an infection episode. Researchers subsequently found *src* in the human genome and the genomes of many other organisms from the fruit fly to the mouse. By 2003, investigators around the world had succeeded in identifying more than 60 oncogenes in the human genome. This information provided, for the first time, a comprehensive theory of cancer induction: Cancers are caused by the conversion of normal cellular genes, known as proto-oncogenes, to oncogenes. Oncogenes have the ability to cause cancer because their normal function is concerned with the regulation of especially important cellular processes, such as regulating the synthesis and repair of DNA, as well as being involved in mediating cell-to-cell communication.

As much as we fear and loathe cancer, this disease has been a driving force behind innumerable studies that have not only led to the discovery of oncogenes but have helped us understand the inner world of the cell. This knowledge has provided us with the ammunition we need to fight cancer but, more importantly, it has paved the way for many powerful therapies that will someday rid the world of other noxious diseases, such as AIDS, Alzheimer's disease, and the infirmities that strike us as we grow old.

This book, another volume in the New Biology set, explores the many facets of cancer research from basic genetic and cellular mechanisms to the influence of lifestyle. The first four chapters introduce cancer terminology and discuss the different types of cancer, the nature of cancer cells, the mechanisms by which normal cells are converted to cancerous cells, and the many changes that occur within a given tissue as cancer progresses. Cancer research has led to many powerful therapies, 10 of which are discussed with reference to their effectiveness as well as the side effects that accompany virtually all of these therapies. Two chapters are devoted to an examination of the influence of environment, diet, and lifestyle on cancer induction and to the success of clinical trials, currently in progress, to treat commonly occurring cancers. The final chapter provides background material on cell biology, recombinant DNA technology, and other topics that are relevant to cancer research.

.1.

COMMON TYPES OF CANCER

In 2003 more than 2 million new cancer cases were diagnosed in the United States alone, and in that same year, more than half a million Americans died of cancer. Cancer can strike anyone, but the risk increases with age, certain lifestyles, and the quality of the environment. Nearly 80 percent of all cancers are diagnosed in patients age 55 and older, and smokers are 20 times more likely to develop lung cancer than nonsmokers. Cancers can appear in any of our tissues and organs, but there are some tissues that are more susceptible than others: Skin cells and the epithelial cells lining the lungs and digestive tract are prominent members in this group. All of these tissues and organs are at the interphase between the external environment and our internal organs, and like a sailor on the mast, take the full force of the storm when it hits (see table on page 3).

The skin is exposed to daily doses of ultraviolet (UV) radiation and a variety of chemicals in the environment. The lungs, while providing us with the oxygen we need to breathe, are exposed to many other gases, such as smoke and pollutants that happen to be in the air. Our digestive tract is in direct contact with the food and water that we consume; and much of what we eat and drink contains chemicals that are often unhealthy, many of which are known carcinogens or mutagens.

Some cancers, such as those affecting the brain, breasts, or prostate gland, do not have clear connections to lifestyle or the environment, but appear to be a consequence of normal physiology and cellular biochemistry. Our bodies, complex machines that they are, simply start to break down after many years, and cancer is one of the regrettable consequences.

The deadliness of a cancer varies depending on the tissue that is affected. Prostate cancer struck more than 200,000 American men in 2003, but the mortality was only 13 percent (that is, 28,900 men died of prostate cancer in the same year). By contrast, brain tumors have a mortality of 72 percent, and lung cancer is even worse, with a mortality of 88 percent. But the deadliest of all cancers are those that appear in the pancreas, where the mortality is a numbing 98 percent (see table on page 3).

The cancers shown in the table, and the seven covered in greater detail later in this chapter, kill millions of people worldwide every year. Brain tumors are described in this chapter, not because they are numerically common, but because of their notoriety, mortality, and the devastating effects they have on the patient's mental faculties.

Terminology

Normal cells become cancerous through a process called *transformation,* leading to the uncontrolled growth of the cancer cells, which produces a *tumor* or *neoplasm.* As long as the tumor remains intact, and the cells do not try to invade other parts of the body, the tumor is called *benign,* and can easily be treated by surgical removal. Tumors become dangerous, and potentially deadly, when some of the cells develop the ability to leave the main tumor mass and migrate to other parts of the body, where they form new tumors; tumors like these are *malignant,* spreading the cancer by a process known as *metastasis.* Malignant cancers can be very difficult, if not impossible, to treat. The danger associated with all tumors is that they will switch from benign to malignant before being detected.

Cancers are classified according to the tissue and cell type from which they arise. Cancers that develop from epithelial cells are called *carcinomas;* those arising from connective tissue or muscles are called *sarcomas;* and those arising from blood-forming tissue, such as the bone marrow, are known as *leukemias.* More than 90 percent of all human cancers are carcinomas.

Cancer names are derived from their cell type, the specific tissue being affected, and whether the tumor is benign or malignant. An *ade-*

NEW CANCER CASES AND DEATHS FOR 2003

Cancer	New Cases	Deaths	Mortality (%)
Bladder	57,400	12,500	22
Brain	18,300	13,100	72
Breast	212,600	40,200	19
Digestive tract	204,400	89,200	44
Leukemia	30,600	21,900	72
Lymphoma	61,000	24,700	41
Liver	17,300	14,400	83
Lung	185,800	163,700	88
Mouth and throat	27,700	7,200	26
Pancreas	30,700	30,000	98
Prostate	220,900	28,900	13
Skin (melanoma)	54,200	7,600	14

Data is for the United States and was compiled from information provided by the American Cancer Society. Mortality is the number of deaths divided by new cases times 100. The values are rounded off to the nearest percentage point.

noma, for example, is a benign tumor originating in the adenoid gland, or other glandular tissue, that consists of epithelial cells. A malignant tumor from the same source is called an *adenocarcinoma.* A *chondroma* is a benign tumor of cartilage, whereas a *chondrosarcoma* is a malignant cartilage tumor. Some cancer names can be real tongue twisters: a type of leukemia that affects blood-forming cells is called *myelocytomatosis.*

Cancers generally retain characteristics that reflect their origin. One type of skin cancer called *basal-cell carcinoma* is derived from keratinocytes and will continue to synthesize keratin, the protein of hair and nails. Another form of skin cancer, called *melanoma,* is derived from pigment cells, and is associated with overproduction of the skin pigment melanin. It is for this reason that these tumors are usually very dark in color. Cancers of the pituitary gland, which produces growth hormone, can lead to production of excessive amounts of this hormone, the effects of which can be more damaging than the cancer itself.

Cancer progression is divided into five stages: *Stage 0* is noninvasive; that is, it has not begun to spread. *Stage I* and *stage II* mark the period when the cancer becomes malignant and begins to spread. At stage I, the tumor is no more than an inch across and the cancer cells have not spread beyond the organ or tissue in which it first appeared. Stage II tumors are still small (one inch or less) but have begun to spread to nearby tissues. A tumor that has increased in size to two inches, but has not begun to spread, is still at stage II. *Stage III* is a locally advanced cancer. In this stage, the tumor is large (more than 2 inches across) and the cancer has spread to nearby tissues. *Stage IV* is metastatic cancer. The cancer has spread to many other tissues and organs of the body. Correct staging is crucial for application of the appropriate therapy.

Bladder Cancer

This cancer is diagnosed in more than 50,000 people every year in the United States alone; it has a moderate mortality of 22 percent and appears to be especially sensitive to diet and the environment.

ANATOMY The bladder is a saclike organ that stores urine from the kidneys. Cancer cells appear in the epithelial cells that line the inside surface of the organ.

RISK FACTORS Bladder cancer is associated with several risk factors, or conditions that increases a person's chance of developing the disease: age, tobacco use, occupation, infections, race, and sex. The chance of getting bladder cancer increases dramatically with age. People under the age of 40 rarely get this disease. Cigarette smokers are six times more likely than nonsmokers to get bladder cancer. Pipe and cigar smokers are also at increased risk. Some workers have a higher risk of getting bladder cancer because of carcinogens in the workplace. Workers in the rubber, chemical, and leather industries are at risk. So are hairdressers, machinists, metalworkers, printers, painters, textile workers, and truck drivers. Being infected with certain tropical parasites increases the risk of developing bladder cancer. Caucasians are twice as likely as African Americans and Hispanics to get bladder cancer. (The lowest rates are among Asians.) Men are two to three times more likely than women to get bladder cancer.

SYMPTOMS Common symptoms of bladder cancer include blood in the urine, pain during urination, and frequent urination, or feeling the need to urinate without results. These are not sure signs of bladder cancer, since other problems, such as bladder stones, can produce similar symptoms.

DIAGNOSIS Bladder cancer is diagnosed with a simple physical exam, to check for obvious tumor growths; a urine test, to check for the presence of blood or cancer cells in the urine; X-ray photography of the bladder; and cystoscopy, whereby a lighted tube is inserted through the urethra to examine the lining of the bladder.

STAGING By stage 0, the cancer cells are found only on the surface of the inner lining of the bladder. This is called superficial cancer or carcinoma in situ. At stage I, the cancer cells are deep in the inner lining of the bladder, and by stage II they have spread to the underlying muscle tissue. By stage III, the cancer cells have spread through the muscular wall of the bladder to the layer of tissue surrounding the bladder. The cancer cells may have spread to the prostate gland (in men) or to the uterus or vagina (in women). By stage IV, the cancer extends to the wall of the abdomen or to the wall of the pelvis. The cancer cells may have spread to lymph nodes, the lungs, and many other parts of the body.

Brain Tumors

Although relatively rare, brain tumors are diagnosed in about 20,000 people in North America every year. Although the number of people affected is small compared with other forms of cancer, brain tumors are included here because they exact an especially heavy toll on those affected. Damage to virtually any area of the brain will leave its mark. Even if the tumor is removed or destroyed, the patient is often left with a lifelong disability.

ANATOMY The brain is divided into three major regions: the cerebrum, the cerebellum (a smaller area located at the lower-back of the brain), and the brain stem, which is continuous with the spinal cord. The brain, along with the spinal cord, is called the central nervous

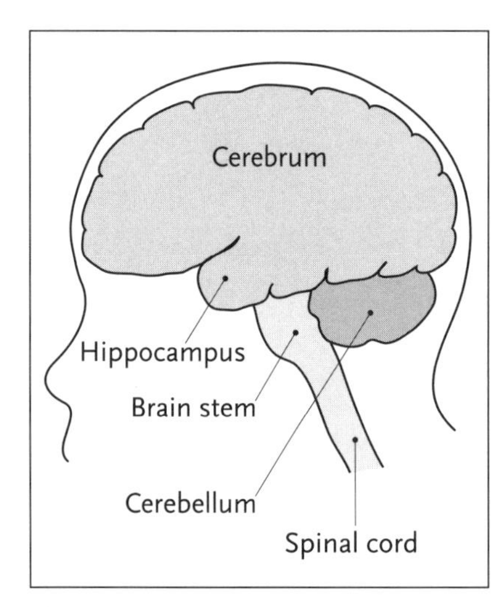

The human central nervous system. The human brain consists of the cerebrum, the cerebellum, and the brain stem, which is continuous with the spinal cord. The brain and spinal cord are called the central nervous system (CNS). The hippocampus, lying beneath the surface of the brain, coordinates memory functions.

system and is constructed of three types of cells: the neurons, the astrocytes (star-shaped) and the oligodendrocytes, the latter two being supportive tissue to the neurons.

The most common brain tumors are gliomas, which originate in the supportive glia tissue: Astrocytomas arise from astrocytes, and may grow anywhere in the brain or spinal cord. In adults, astrocytomas most often arise in the cerebrum. In children, they occur in the brain stem, the cerebrum, and the cerebellum. Brain stem gliomas occur in the lowest, stemlike part of the brain, where they are difficult, if not impossible, to remove. Oligodendrogliomas arise in the glia cells that produce myelin, the fatty covering that protects nerves. These tumors usually arise in the cerebrum; they grow slowly and usually do not spread into surrounding brain tissue.

Brain tumors occur most often in middle-aged adults and are frequently secondary tumors; that is, tumors that originated in some other part of the body. Secondary tumors are named after the tissue of their origin. For example, a brain tumor that originated in the lung is called metastatic lung cancer, and the cells from such a tumor will resemble lung tissue, not neurons or glia cells.

RISK FACTORS The patient's age is the dominant risk factor. There is no clear link with lifestyle or environmental pollutants. Some people have suspected exposure to cell phone radiation, but this has not been proven, and several attempts to do so have met with failure.

SYMPTOMS The effect that tumors have upon the brain depends primarily on their size and location. Growing tumors may put pressure on surrounding tissue, damaging neurons and the many connections they make with other cells. Swelling and a buildup of fluid around the tumor also cause damage to the brain, a condition called edema. Tumors can also block the flow of cerebrospinal fluid, causing it to build up inside the brain, producing a condition known as hydrocephalus. Common symptoms of brain tumors include the following: headaches that tend to be worse in the morning and ease during the day; seizures (convulsions); nausea or vomiting; weakness or loss of feeling in the

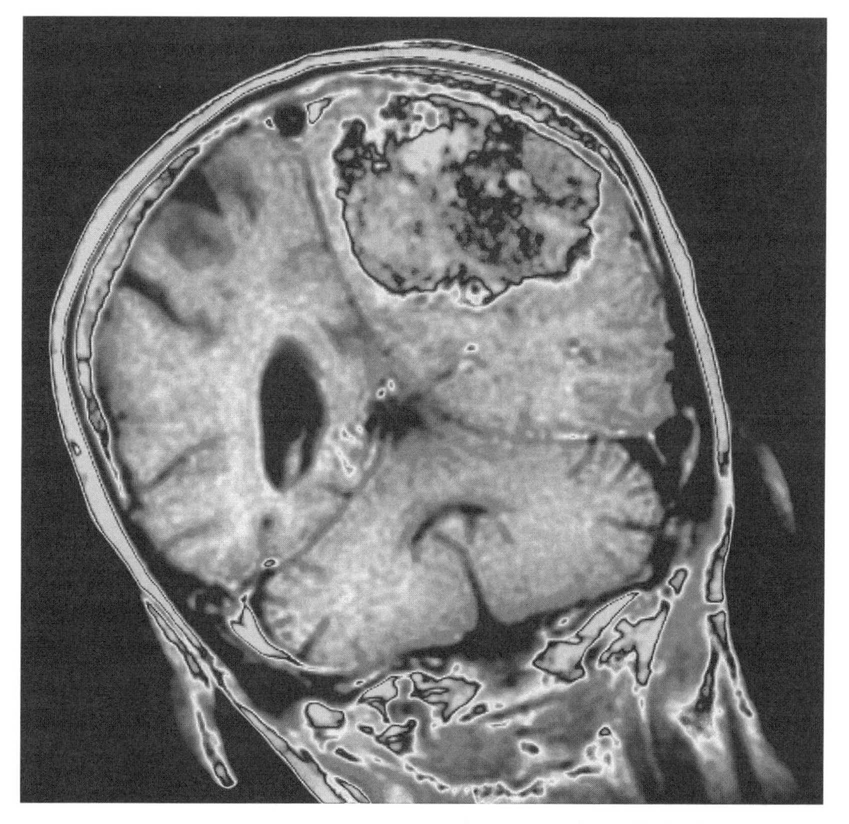

Magnetic resonance imaging (MRI) scan of a section through the brain of a 74-year-old woman showing a large tumor (upper right cerebral hemisphere). Brain tumors may arise in the brain or they may develop from cancers arising elsewhere in the body. *(Simon Fraser/SPL/Photo Researchers, Inc.)*

arms or legs; stumbling or lack of coordination in walking; abnormal eye movements or changes in vision; persistent drowsiness; changes in personality, memory, or speech habits.

DIAGNOSIS Brain tumors are diagnosed primarily with a computed tomography (CT) scan or with magnetic resonance imaging (MRI). A CT scan is a series of detailed pictures of the brain that are created by a computer linked to an X-ray machine. In some cases, a special dye is injected into a vein before the scan, which increases tissue contrast. MRI produces computerized pictures of the brain that are based on the magnetic properties of the molecules in the tissue. A special dye may be used to enhance the likelihood of detecting a brain tumor.

STAGING Brain tumors rarely metastasize to other tissues or organs, but simply grow at their point of origin. Since damage to any part of the CNS is likely to have serious consequences, the main concern with a brain tumor is how fast it is growing. For these reasons, standard staging is not used. Instead, brain tumors are referred to as low, intermediate or high grade, with respect to their growth rate.

Breast Cancer

Other than lung and colon cancer, breast cancer is the most common type of cancer among women in North America, where more than 200,000 cases are diagnosed each year. Breast cancer also affects more than 2,000 men each year.

ANATOMY Each breast has 15 to 20 sections called lobes. Within each lobe are many smaller lobules. Lobules end in dozens of tiny bulbs that can produce milk. Thin tubes, called ducts, link all the lobes, lobules, and bulbs. These ducts lead to the nipple in the center of a dark area of skin called the areola. There are no muscles in the breast, but muscles lie under each breast and cover the ribs. The breasts also contain blood vessels and vessels for the lymphatic system, which consists of many lymph nodes found throughout the body. Many lymph nodes are found near the breast, under the arm, above the collarbone, and in the chest. The most common type of breast cancer is ductal carcinoma, which begins in the lining of the ducts. The second type occurs in the lobes and is called lobular carcinoma.

RISK FACTORS There are three major risk factors associated with both forms of breast cancer: mutations in two genes (BRCA1 and BRCA2), estrogen exposure, and late childbearing. The breast cancer genes 1 and 2 code for proteins that are needed to correct errors in DNA synthesis during the cell cycle. Estrogen is responsible for stimulating the breasts as part of normal reproductive physiology but over time may lead to the transformation of the duct cells. The connection between late childbearing and breast cancer is not clear.

SYMPTOMS There is no pain or discomfort associated with the early stages of breast cancer, which may produce a lump or thickening in or near the breast or in the underarm area; a change in the size or shape of the breast; nipple discharge or tenderness; or swelling, redness, or scaling of the skin of the breast, areola, or nipple.

DIAGNOSIS Breast cancers are diagnosed with a clinical breast exam, mammography, ultrasonography, and biopsy. The clinical exam is used to locate obvious lumps in the breast. It is often possible to tell if a lump is benign or malignant by the way it feels, how easily it moves, and its texture. Mammography uses X-rays to obtain a picture of the breast and any lumps that may be present. Ultrasonography uses high-frequency sound waves to determine whether a lump is a fluid-filled cyst (not cancer) or a solid mass (which may or may not be cancer). This exam may be used along with mammography. In some case, samples of a suspected tumor are obtained so the cells may be examined under a microscope. This procedure is referred to as a biopsy, and the tissue sample is usually collected with a hypodermic needle.

STAGING Stage 0 is noninvasive carcinoma. By stage I or II, the cancer has spread beyond the lobe or duct and invaded nearby tissue. At stage I the tumor is no more than an inch across, and the cancer cells are still inside the breast. Cancer cells begin to spread to underarm (axillary) lymph nodes by stage II. If the tumor increases in size to two inches but has not spread, it is still at stage II. Stage III is locally

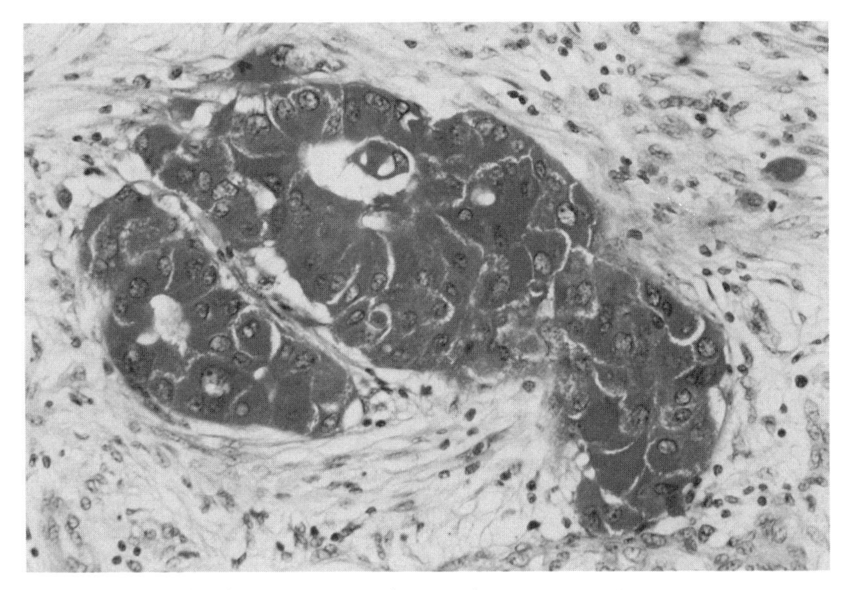

Light micrograph of a carcinoma in human breast tissue. A carcinoma is a malignant tumor arising from cells in the surface layer or lining tissue of a body organ. *(Michael Abbey/Photo Researchers, Inc.)*

advanced cancer. The tumor is more than two inches across and the cancer has spread to the axillary lymph nodes and other nearby tissues. By stage IV, the cancer has spread beyond the breast to many other parts of the body.

Leukemia

Each year, nearly 32,000 adults and more than 2,000 children in the United States learn that they have leukemia, a cancer of the blood cells.

ANATOMY There are three different types of blood cells: red blood cells (RBC or erythrocytes), white blood cells (WBC, or leukocytes), and platelets (thrombocytes). Red blood cells contain hemoglobin and use it to carry oxygen from the lungs to the tissues. White blood cells do not carry oxygen but are part of the body's immune system. White blood cells are either lymphocytes (spend much of their time in the lymphatic system) or myeloid cells (spend much of their time in the bone marrow or general circulation). Platelets are not complete cells but are fragments of certain kinds of leukocytes, and they are involved in blood clotting.

Leukemia affects white blood cells only and can arise in either lymphoid cells (lymphocytic leukemia) or myeloid cells (myelogenous leukemia). The disease has two forms: acute and chronic leukemia. Acute leukemia is a devastating disease that progresses very quickly, destroying the patient's immune system. Chronic leukemia progresses much more slowly, and even though the leukocytes are transforming, they retain some of their normal functions, so the immune system is not destroyed so quickly, or so completely.

RISK FACTORS The patient's age is the primary risk factor. Acute lymphocytic leukemia is the most common type of leukemia in young children and in adults who are 65 and older. Acute myeloid leukemia (also called acute nonlymphocytic leukemia) occurs in both adults and children. Chronic lymphocytic leukemia most often affects adults over the age of 55. It sometimes occurs in younger adults, but rarely affects children. Chronic myeloid leukemia occurs mainly in adults. Very few children ever develop this form of leukemia.

SYMPTOMS Some symptoms of leukemia are fever, chills, and other flulike symptoms; weakness and fatigue; frequent infections; loss of appetite and/or weight; swollen or tender lymph nodes, liver, or spleen; easy bleeding or bruising; tiny red spots under the skin; swollen or bleeding gums; sweating, especially at night; and/or bone or joint pain. Leukemia metastasizing to the brain may cause headaches, vomiting, confusion, loss of muscle control, and seizures. Leukemia cells can also colonize the testicles, where they cause pain and swelling; the skin and eyes, where they produce sores; and many other organs and tissues of the body.

DIAGNOSIS The patient is examined for swelling in the liver, the spleen, and the lymph nodes under the arms, in the groin, and in the neck. A blood sample is examined under the microscope to check for abnormal white blood cells. The most definitive test is the microscopic examination of a bone marrow biopsy, which is obtained by inserting a needle into the hip and removing a small amount of bone marrow. If

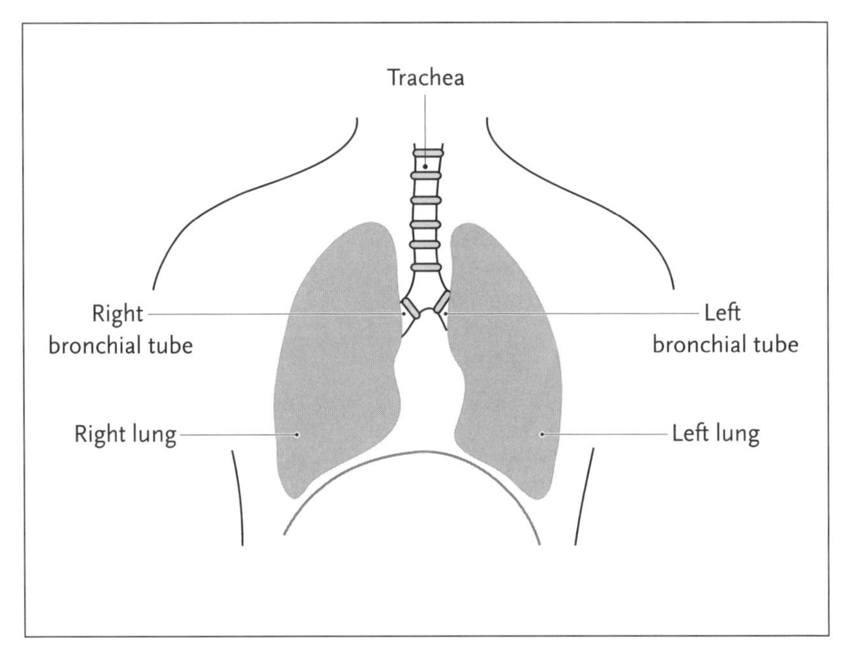

The lungs are part of the respiratory system and fill most of the thoracic cavity. The trachea divides into two bronchial tubes, each of which branch out like a tree inside the lung. The branches are called bronchioles and terminate in grapelike clusters of alveoli, where gas exchange occurs between the air and the blood.

cancer cells are found, X-rays are obtained to evaluate the spread of the disease.

STAGING Staging is difficult to determine with this form of cancer, since the leukocytes normally travel throughout the body. Consequently, transformation and metastasis may occur simultaneously.

Lung Cancer

This cancer is very common and very deadly. More than 180,000 cases are diagnosed every year in the United States alone, and of these, nearly 90 percent die of the disease. Although it is one of the most deadly of all cancers, it is also the most preventable.

ANATOMY The lungs are a pair of cone-shaped organs that are part of the respiratory system. The right lung has three sections, called lobes, and is a little larger than the left lung, which has two lobes. When we breathe, the lungs take in oxygen, which our cells need to live and carry out their normal functions. When we exhale, the lungs get rid of carbon dioxide, a cellular waste product. Most lung cancers start in the epithelial lining of the bronchi, and occasionally in the trachea, bronchioles, or alveoli. All forms of lung cancer, being derived from epithelial cells, are carcinomas.

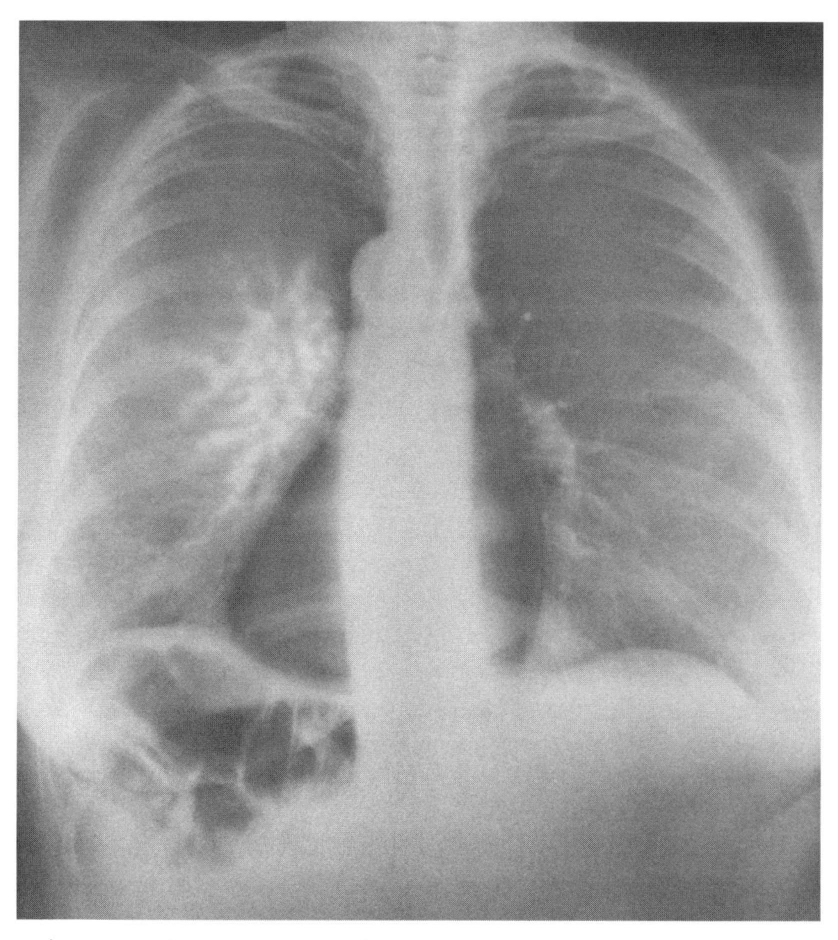

A chest X-ray showing evidence of cancer in the right lung. *(Chris Bjornberg/ Photo Researchers, Inc.)*

RISK FACTORS Scientists have discovered several causes of lung cancer, most due to atmospheric pollutants and the use of tobacco. The smoke from cigarettes, cigars, and pipes contains many compounds called carcinogens that can damage cells, leading to the formation of cancer. The likelihood that a smoker will develop lung cancer is affected by the age at which smoking began, how long the person has smoked, the number of cigarettes smoked per day, and how deeply the smoker inhales. Stopping smoking greatly reduces a person's risk for developing lung cancer. Environmental tobacco smoke, or secondhand smoke, is just as dangerous. Work-related exposure to radioactive gases, such as radon, and to asbestos dust is also known to cause cancer. Atmospheric pollutants, contributed by car and truck exhaust, are also believed to be risk factors, but the link is not proven.

SYMPTOMS Symptoms of lung cancer include a cough that doesn't go away and gets worse over time; constant chest pain; coughing up blood; shortness of breath, wheezing, or hoarseness; repeated problems with pneumonia or bronchitis; swelling of the neck and face; loss of appetite or weight loss and chronic fatigue.

DIAGNOSIS A chest X-ray to visualize possible tumors, and a lung biopsy are the most common methods used to diagnose lung cancer.

STAGING Lung cancer usually spreads to the brain and bones. CT scans and MRI are the most common methods for determining the stage of this form of cancer.

Prostate Cancer

Prostate cancer is the most common type of cancer in North American men. The number of men affected by prostate cancer is nearly equal to the number of women affected by breast cancer, but the mortality of prostate cancer is lower (see table on page 3).

ANATOMY The prostate gland is part of the male reproductive system. It makes and stores portions of the seminal fluid, a fluid that is mixed with sperm to produce semen. The gland is about the size of a walnut and is located below the bladder near the base of the penis. It surrounds the upper part of the urethra, the tube that empties urine from the bladder. Because of its location, abnormal growth of the prostate can pinch the urethra, blocking the flow of urine. The prostate gland is regulated by the male sex hormone, testosterone.

RISK FACTORS Age, family history, and diet are the main risk factors. Prostate cancer usually occurs in men over the age of 55. The average age of patients at the time of diagnosis is 70. A man's risk of developing prostate cancer is higher if his father or brother has had the disease. This disease is much more common in African-American men than in white men. It is less common in Asian and American Indian men. Some evidence suggests that a diet high in animal fat may increase the risk of prostate cancer and a diet high in fruits and vegetables may decrease the risk. Studies are in progress to learn whether men can reduce their risk of prostate cancer by taking certain dietary supplements.

SYMPTOMS Common symptoms of prostate cancer are a need to urinate frequently, especially at night; difficulty starting urination or holding back urine; inability to urinate; weak or interrupted flow of urine; painful or burning urination; difficulty in having an erection; painful ejaculation; blood in urine or semen; or, in advanced stages, frequent pain or stiffness in the lower back, hips, or upper thighs.

DIAGNOSIS Digital rectal exam (DRE) and a blood test for prostate-specific antigen (PSA) are the methods used to diagnose prostate cancer. The patient's doctor inserts a lubricated, gloved finger into the rectum and feels the prostate through the rectal wall to check for hard or lumpy areas. The diagnosis, based on this simple procedure, is surprisingly accurate and informative. Confirmation of cancer, based on the DRE, is obtained by testing the patient's blood for the presence of PSA. PSA is a semen protein produced by the prostate, and under normal circumstances it should never appear in the blood. Blood that is positive for PSA is strong evidence of prostate cancer. This test is sometimes followed up with a biopsy and ultrasonography.

STAGING At stage I, the tumor cannot be felt during a rectal exam and there is no evidence that it has spread beyond the prostate. At stage II, the tumor is large enough to be felt during a rectal exam, but is still noninvasive. By stage III, the cancer has spread outside the prostate to nearby tissues, and at stage IV, cancer cells have colonized the lymph nodes and many other parts of the body.

Skin Cancer

This is the most common type of cancer in North America, with 1 million cases being diagnosed each year. The table on page 3 shows data only for melanoma. Nearly half of the North American population will develop some form of skin cancer by age 65. Although anyone can get skin cancer, the risk is greatest for people who have fair skin that freckles easily, often those with red or blond hair and blue or light-colored eyes.

ANATOMY The skin protects us against heat, light, injury, and infection. It helps regulate body temperature and stores water, fat, and vitamin D. The skin is made up of two main layers: the outer epidermis and the inner dermis. The epidermis is mostly made up of flat, scalelike cells called squamous cells. Under the squamous cells are round cells called basal cells. The deepest part of the epidermis also contains melanocytes, cells that produce melanin, which gives the skin its color. The dermis (just below the epidermis) contains blood and lymph vessels, hair follicles, and glands. These glands produce sweat to regulate body temperature and sebum, an oily substance that helps keep the skin from drying out. Sweat and sebum reach the skin's surface through tiny openings called pores.

The two most common kinds of skin cancer are basal cell carcinoma and squamous cell carcinoma. Basal cell carcinoma accounts for more than 90 percent of all skin cancers in North America. It is a slow-growing cancer that seldom spreads to other parts of the body. Squamous cell carcinoma also rarely spreads, but it does so more often than basal cell carcinoma. Another type of cancer that occurs in the skin is melanoma, which begins in the melanocytes. Melanomas are quick to metastasize and are often deadly. Basal cell carcinoma and squamous cell carcinoma are sometimes called nonmelanoma skin cancer.

RISK FACTORS The primary risk factor is excessive exposure to ultraviolet radiation. The use of sunscreens (particularly on children), hats, and protective clothing are strongly recommended for lengthy outdoor excursions.

SYMPTOMS The most common warning sign of skin cancer is a growth or a sore that does not heal. Skin cancers vary considerably in the way they look. Some begin as a pale waxy lump, whereas others first appear as a firm red lump. Sometimes; the lump bleeds or develops a crust. Skin cancer can also start as a flat, red spot that is rough, dry, or

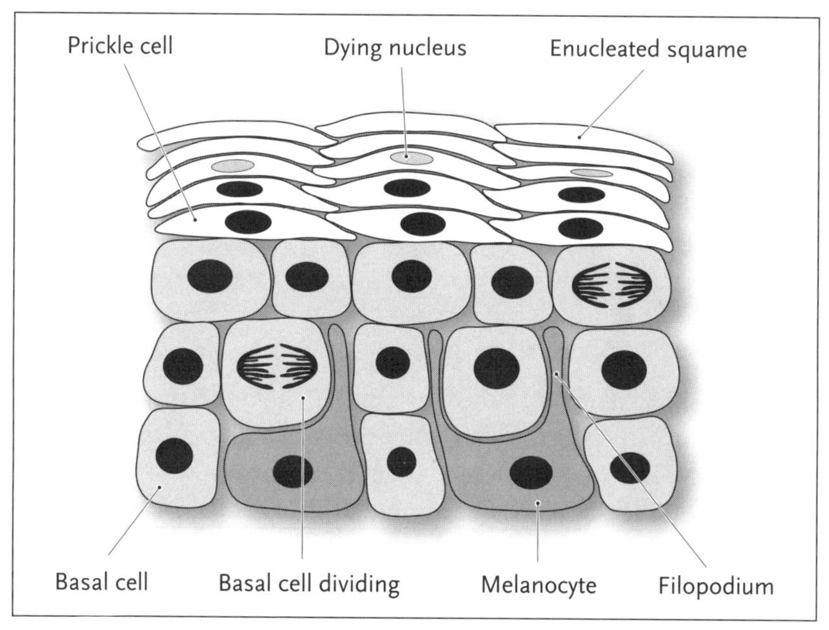

The epidermis is a stratified epithelium that forms the outer layer of the skin. It consists of three cell populations: squamous cells (the enucleated squames and the prickle cells), the cuboidal basal cells, and, at the deepest layers, pigment-containing melanocytes. The basal and squamous cell layers are in a constant state of change. Division of a basal cell is followed by keratinization, a process by which the daughter cells are transformed into prickle cells. Keratin is a tough protein that makes the outer cell layer resistant to abrasion. In the final stage of keratinization, the prickle cell loses its nucleus and the now dead and fully keratinized squame eventually flakes off from the surface. Keratinized squames from the scalp are called dandruff.

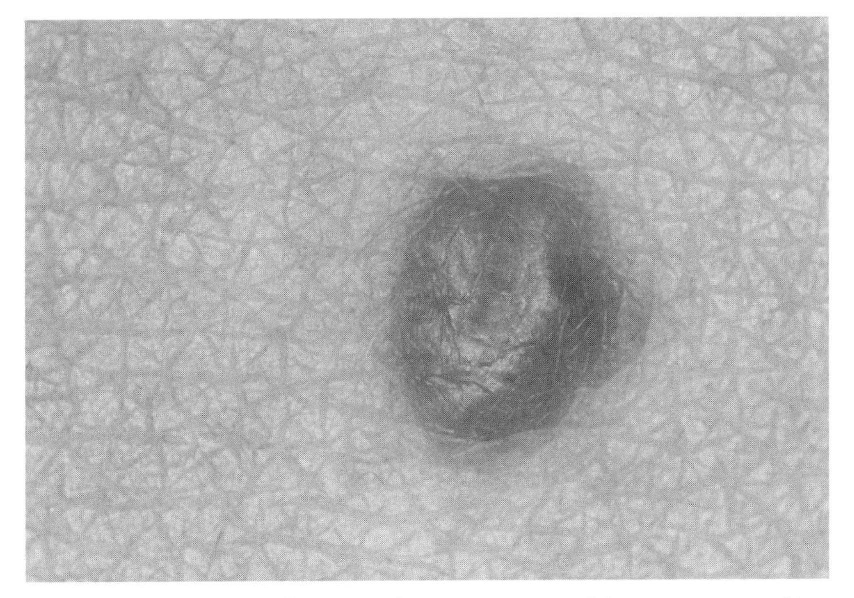

Juvenile melanoma. A malignant melanoma is a type of skin cancer caused by tumors arising in melanocytes. These cancers usually start as moles and are caused by mutations induced by overexposure to ultraviolet radiation in sunlight. They can be fatal if not treated early. *(Biophoto Associates/Photo Researchers, Inc.)*

scaly. Both basal and squamous cell cancers are found on areas of the skin that are often exposed to the sun: the face, neck, hands, and arms. Actinic keratosis, which appears as rough red or brown scaly patches on the skin, is known as a precancerous condition because it sometimes develops into squamous cell cancer.

DIAGNOSIS Basal and squamous cell carcinomas are generally diagnosed and treated in the same way. When an area of skin does not look normal, all or part of the growth is removed and a portion of the biopsy will be examined under a microscope.

STAGING Basal and squamous cell carcinoma rarely spread beyond the skin. Melanoma, however, can metastasize to other tissues and organs. CT and MRI are commonly used to assess the invasiveness of malignant melanoma.

.2.
CANCER CELLS

What happens to a cell when it becomes cancerous, when it loses its identity and stops caring about the community that it lives in? When Robert Louis Stevenson wrote *The Strange Case of Dr. Jekyll and Mr. Hyde,* in 1886, he was trying to illustrate the complex nature of the human psyche, which seems to be a mixture of good and bad intentions. Dr. Jekyll was a good and honest man, but his experiments turned him into the very bad Mr. Hyde, a crazy man who cared for nothing. Today, we know that human insanity can be traced to a disturbance in brain biochemistry. Likewise, the insanity of a cancer cell can now be traced to a disturbance in the biochemistry of the cell cycle and cellular communication. A deranged cell cycle can sometimes have a dramatic effect on a cell's lifespan.

Cancer Cells Are Immortal

The difference between cancer cells and normal cells is profound, not only because of the way they look and the way they behave, but because of the radical difference in their lifespans. Placed in tissue culture, cancer cells can live forever. Normal cells, on the other hand, die after about 50 generations. The best proof of cancer cell immortality comes from HeLa cells, a cultured cancer cell line that was established in 1951 from a cervical tumor that was isolated from a woman named Henrietta Lacks. The HeLa cell line has been growing well ever since, and cultures of these cells are maintained for research purposes by laboratories around to world. Henrietta Lacks, a native of Baltimore, Maryland, was 31 years old when the tumor was discovered. She died of cervical cancer eight months later.

It may seem odd to think that the achievement of immortality is a bad thing. There is a tendency to believe that if a cell becomes immortal, it might immortalize the entire organism. But an animal's body is designed around the principle of regulated cell division for the good of the community. Most cells in an adult's body are postmitotic, a condition that guarantees a stable organ size and shape. Some cells, such as skin and bone marrow, are allowed to divide, but only a limited number of times. The only immortal cells in the body are the germ cells (sperm and eggs), although even they will die out if the individual never has children. This is not to say that such an arrangement can never be tampered with. Stem cells can also proliferate for years in culture (although we do not yet know if they are truly immortal) and their use in medical therapies may make it possible to extend the human lifespan, but for now, the acquisition of immortality by a somatic cell always leads to trouble.

For 40 years scientists struggled to understand the mechanism by which cancer cells are immortalized. Throughout the 1990s attention was drawn to a special DNA sequence called a telomere, located at the

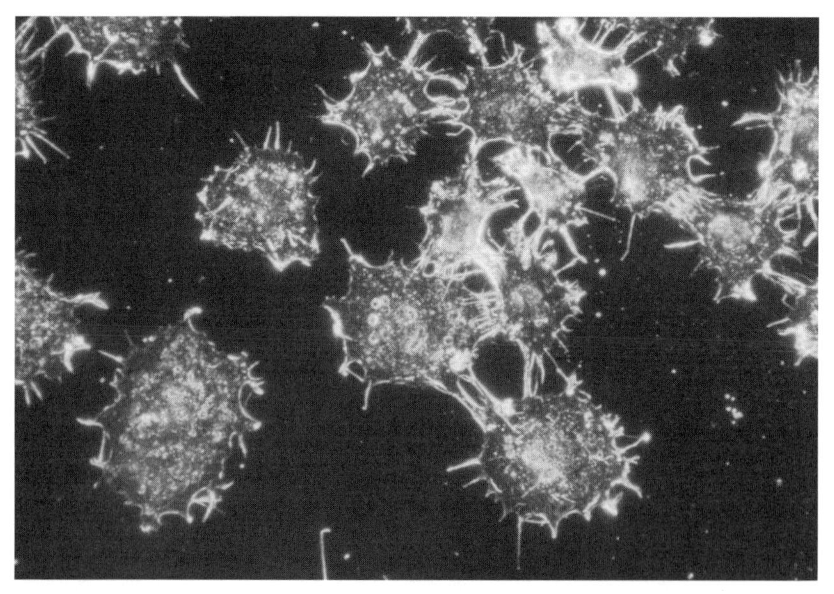

Cultured human carcinoma cells showing the very irregular surface membrane. *(Dr. Cecil H. Fox/Photo Researchers, Inc.)*

tips of the chromosomes. Each time the DNA is replicated during the S phase (see chapter 3) of the cell cycle, the telomeres shrink, but they are later restored by a special enzyme called telomerase. By carefully studying the mechanics of DNA replication, scientists have been able to conclude that telomeres are essential for the correct duplication of each chromosome. A failure to duplicate the DNA automatically terminates the cell cycle. Normal cells lack telomerase (that is, the gene for telomerase is turned off in adult cells), and for this reason they cannot proliferate indefinitely in the body (in vivo) or in cell culture (in vitro).

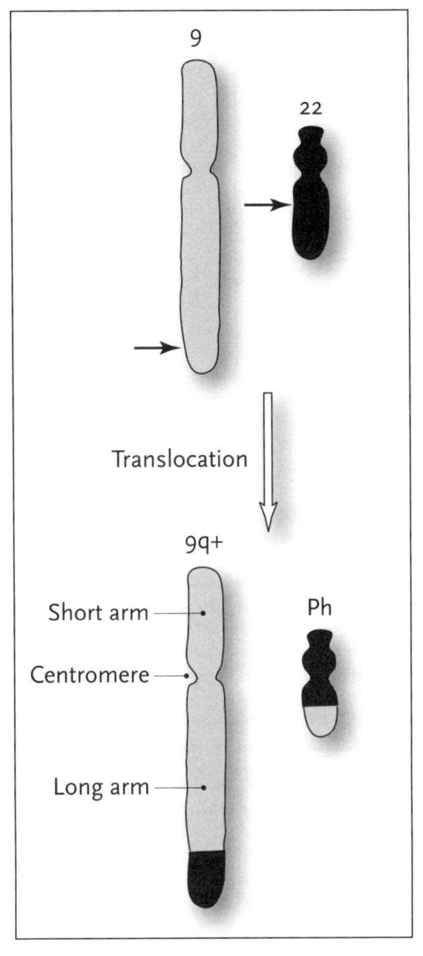

The Philadelphia chromosome (Ph) is produced by a translocation between the long arms of chromosomes 9 and 22. The short arrows mark the fragmentation points. The chromosomes are aligned at the centromeres.

Broken Chromosomes

Becoming immortal is only one of many things that must happen before a cell becomes cancerous. A cell that simply divides indefinitely can produce a tumor mass, but as long as it remains benign it can usually be removed surgically. The real danger occurs when some of the cancer cells break away from the original tumor to colonize other parts of the body. Metastasis is a complex process that involves many changes in the cell's biochemistry. The earliest indication that these changes are rooted in the cell's genes came

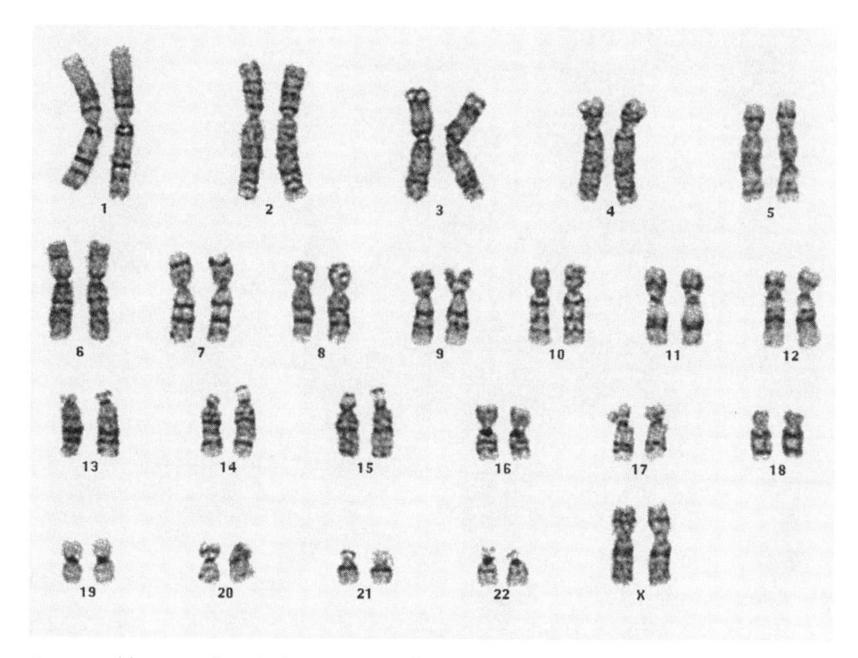

A normal human female karyotype. A karyotype represents the full set of chromosomes arranged with respect to size, shape, and number. Human cells contain 23 pairs of chromosomes: 22 autosomes and a pair of sex chromosomes. The sex chromosomes are either X or Y. Females have two X chromosomes, whereas males have an X and a Y chromosome. Karyotypes are used to diagnose genetic illnesses and are also used to characterize different forms of cancer. *(Courtesy of Diana Dowsley)*

from histological examinations of cancer cells. These studies showed that most cancer cells have an abnormal karyotype that is characterized by the presence of many broken chromosomes.

The Philadelphia chromosome (named after the city where it was first discovered) is a striking example of the relationship between genetic abnormality and cancer induction. This chromosomal abnormality involves a translocation between the long arms of chromosomes 9 and 22. This abnormality is associated with chronic myelogenous leukemia and can be found in the leukemic white blood cells of virtually every patient suffering from this form of cancer. The Philadelphia chromosome alters the normal gene expression of the cell and is one example of a somatic mutation, or change in the genome, that can lead to cancer.

A Failure to Communicate

When normal cells are placed in culture they can proliferate long enough to cover the bottom of the dish in a single layer, or monolayer, of cells. When the monolayer is established, the cells stop growing due to a phenomenon known as contact inhibition. The cells in the monolayer know they are in contact with other cells and this information is enough to signal an end to proliferation, to ensure that the cells do not pile up on each other. Cancer cells, in culture, do not respond to contact inhibition. Instead, they continue growing, often forming large clumps of cells on the plate.

The failure of contact inhibition in cancer cells is a failure to communicate, and is due to an abnormal glycocalyx. In normal cells, the glycocalyx contains many cell surface glycoproteins that act like sensory antennae. When those antennae make contact with the glycocalyx of another cell, the information is relayed to the interior of the cell by

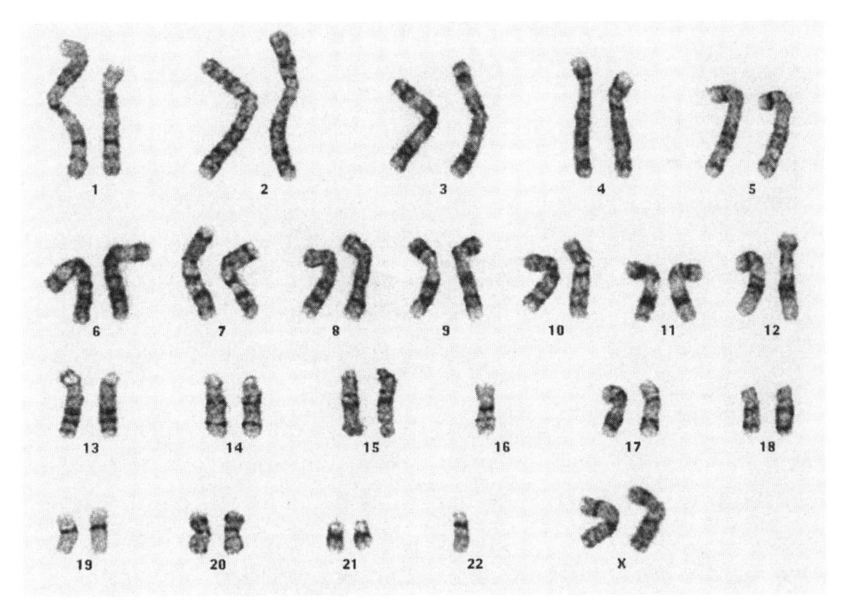

An abnormal human female karyotype. This karyotype is typical of a cancer known as Whilm's carcinoma, which is characterized by three deletions: a partial deletion of chromosome 1 and total deletions of chromosomes 16 and 22. *(Courtesy of Diana Dowsley)*

a signaling pathway that tells the cell to stop growing. It may also activate other pathways that stimulate the formation of physical connections between the cells. None of this works in cancer cells. The antennae are either gone or are no longer linked to the proper signaling pathway. As a consequence, cancer cells grow over the top of one another, and the only thing that limits their growth, in vivo and in vitro, is the availability of oxygen and nutrients. As they pile up, forming a large clump, the cells in the middle stop dividing and may even die for want of food and air.

They Go Where They Please

The corrupted communication channels that are characteristic of cancer cells account for their apparent lack of manners and their tendency to crowd each other when grown in culture; it also accounts for the ability of cancer cells to colonize tissues that are normally reserved for other cells. A normal heart cell would never try to colonize the brain or the liver. Conversely, brain cells would never try to invade the skin, bone, or any other type of tissue.

If a normal cell should accidentally break loose from its parent tissue or organ and find itself in foreign territory, it would quickly receive and process signals from the surrounding cells that would cause it to commit suicide. Cell suicide is called apoptosis, and it is regulated by specific communication pathways. Cancer cells will not commit suicide. They either ignore the signals from cells around them, or the pathways regulating apoptosis are dysfunctional. In either case, the loss of the death signal makes it possible for cancer cells to grow in any environment.

However, the ability to ignore an order to commit suicide is only one element in the complex process known as metastasis. For cancer cells to invade other territory, they must break loose from the tumor mass, travel through the tissue or organ until they reach a blood vessel, penetrate the vessel wall, and then, after being carried along in the circulating blood, exit the vessel in some other part of the body. Once they have colonized fresh territory and begin forming a tumor they must activate angiogenesis, the growth of blood vessels into the tumor, in order to receive oxygen and nutrients. This may appear to be an unlikely scenario, depending as it does on so many processes, but cancer cells are capable of coordinating all of these events, and when they do, they are free to go where they please.

One Mutation Is Not Enough

Cancer cells are genetic mutants; this is clear from their abnormal karyotype and the apparent distortions in their communication pathways. These changes produce a standard behavior pattern for cancer cells that consists of the following:

- They ignore signals that regulate proliferation.
- They sidestep built-in limitations to their own reproduction.
- They are genetically unstable.
- They escape their parent tissue.
- They colonize foreign tissue.
- They avoid suicide.

This list is a good indication that more than one defective gene is required to produce a cancer cell. The actual number of genetic mutations that must occur to produce a cancer cell is unknown, but may involve 10 to 20 genes. The mutations occur slowly over time in a sequential fashion and may account for the age-related onset of brain tumors, breast cancer, and prostate cancer. This fits with many observations over the past 10 years concerning tumor progression, whereby a mildly abnormal cell gives rise to a colony of cells that gradually evolves into metastatic cancer.

The driving force behind the evolution of a cancer appears to be the genetic instability that is characteristic of these cells. Normal cells are vigilant and constantly check the accuracy of their products by monitoring the behavior of their own machinery. When the DNA is duplicated in preparation for cell division, regulators, monitors, and repair enzymes are on guard to make sure no mistakes occurred when the daughter strand was made. If an error is detected, the cell does not divide until the damage is repaired. If the damage cannot be repaired, the cell will either commit suicide voluntarily or be forced to do so by the immune system. Repair enzymes and monitors also check to ensure the chromosomes segregate properly (that is, are portioned out equally to the daughter cells). If segregation is abnormal, one daughter cell will end up with too many chromosomes, while the other cell will have too few. When this happens, apoptosis is activated by the monitoring system, so that both cells commit suicide.

Cancer cells behave as though they have an absolute disdain for quality control. If an error is made during DNA synthesis, they do not bother making repairs before continuing through the cell cycle. If chromosomes fail to segregate normally or develop an abnormal karyotype, the two daughter cells do not commit suicide. In this way, the abnormal cell line accumulates many genetic abnormalities until it becomes malignant, or until it is destroyed by the immune system. In a bizarre sense, cancer cells are trying to establish a situation in which genetic variability is maximized, with a subsequent increase in the rate at which they evolve.

The accumulation of mutations through genetic instability is acted upon by natural selection. Most of the cells in the original tumor will be so abnormal they will be incapable of providing for themselves and will eventually die out. In many cases this will lead to the disappearance of the entire tumor mass. But it can also happen that an abnormal cell will appear within the original tumor that has just the right combination of mutated genes, mutations that turn a benign tumor into a malignant cancer.

·3·

THE ROAD TO ONCOGENESIS

What could cells have been thinking, all those long years as they climbed out the primordial ooze to produce the stunning array of creatures that now inhabit the Earth? They dealt with obstacles that would have killed the faint of heart, noxious atmospheres that would make us choke, heat that would curl or straighten our hair, and storms that would make us quake in our boots. All these hurdles were brushed aside, like a bit of dust in the air, as cells refined their structure and expanded their communities to such an extent that they tamed the Earth and made its atmosphere fit for modern creatures to breathe.

But all along, as they went from one triumph to the next, their free-living carefree lifestyle set the stage for trouble to come. Oncogenesis (cancer development) is an unfortunate legacy of our protozoan ancestry. Paradoxically, cancer as we know it does not exist for modern-day protozoans. If any of those cells becomes abnormal, it is of no great consequence; that crazy cell, with a mangled genetic composition, simply dies because of its weirdness, without taking a virtual universe of cells with it. Perhaps this is why our single-cell ancestors never found a way to fully protect themselves from cancer: it simply did not matter to them. Abnormal cells occurred, but they never threatened the survival of other cells.

Our protozoan ancestors were not only free-living, but like economists, they were firm believers in the principle of continual growth. Those cells never became postmitotic but divided every half-hour or so and kept it up for as long as they could. To this extent, protozoans and their bacterial ancestors are immortal creatures that have existed for millions of years. But in order to produce multicellular organisms, protozoans had to come to some kind of mutual understanding, which limited the reproductive ability of some of the cells, forcing them to become postmitotic, while allowing others to divide for the life of the organism.

For the postmitotic crowd, the arrangement may have seemed impossible, as they were being asked to do something that went against their very nature. Genes that regulated their reproduction, which had undergone millions of years of adaptive evolution to ensure the cells could divide rapidly, were now being asked to shut down and remain silent. For the mitotic crowd, the agreement meant that each cell division had to be tightly controlled; no variation in the daughter cells would be allowed as it might have been with their free-living ancestors. When a human cell becomes cancerous it is simply reawakening its ancestral urge for unlimited growth and the carefree attitude that comes with it. The immortal lifestyle of protozoans depends on special genes that regulate the cell cycle and communication with the outside world. In that context, those genes are the cell's most prized possession, but when a cell in an animal's body becomes cancerous, those same cherished genes begin to fail and ultimately become a liability.

Cancer and the Cell Cycle

Evolution of cells has always been marked by two competing forces: the need for change, so the cell can evolve, and the need to stay the same, so daughter cells can inherit whatever genetic advantage the parent cell had. In the short term, cells work a very long day to make sure their daughter cells are as much like the original as possible. Cell cycle monitors, consisting of many different enzymes, check to make sure that everything is going well each time a cell divides, and if it is not, those monitors stop the cell from dividing until the problem is corrected. If the damage cannot be repaired, a protozoan remains stuck in midstream for the remainder of its life. If this happens to a cell in an animal's body, the cell is forced to commit suicide, in a process called apoptosis, by other cells in the immediate neighborhood or by the immune system.

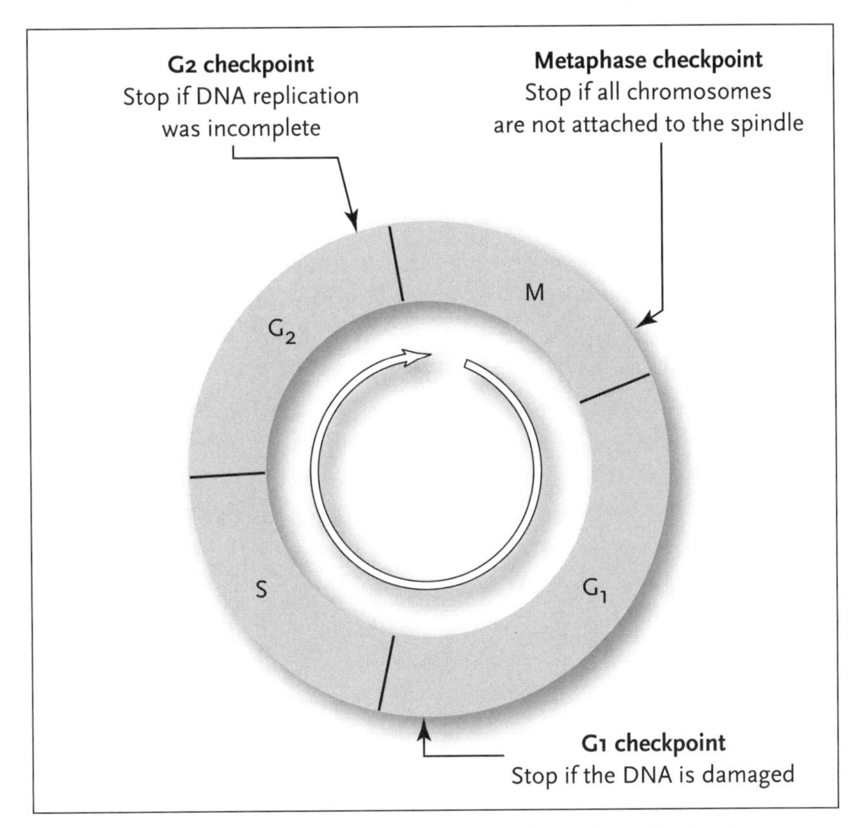

Cell cycle checkpoints. The cell cycle is equipped with three checkpoints to ensure that the daughter cells are identical and that there is no genetic damage. The circular arrow indicates the direction of the cycle.

The cell cycle consists of four stages or phases: cell division (M phase, for mitosis); a gap immediately after M phase, called G_1; DNA synthesis (S phase); followed by another gap, called G_2. The cycle includes three checkpoints: the first is a DNA damage checkpoint that occurs in G_1. The monitors check for damage that may have occurred as a result of the last cell cycle or were caused by something in the environment, such as UV radiation or toxic chemicals. If damage is detected, DNA synthesis is blocked until it can be repaired. The second checkpoint occurs in G_2, where the monitors make sure errors were not introduced when the chromosomes were duplicated during the S phase. The G_1 and G_2 checkpoints are sometimes referred to collectively as

DNA damage checkpoints. The third and final checkpoint occurs in M phase, to ensure that all of the chromosomes are properly attached to the spindle. This checkpoint is intended to prevent gross abnormalities in the daughter cells with regard to chromosome number. If a chromosome fails to attach to the spindle, one daughter cell will end up with too many chromosomes, while the other will have too few.

Typically, cancer cells lose one or more of their checkpoint monitors, so they divide whether things are right or not. This is the reason they develop an abnormal genome and physical appearance. Corrupting the genome in this way may seem to spell certain death for a cell, but it is really the means by which cancer cells reinvent themselves. The checkpoints are intended to maintain the status quo; without them the genetic profile of a cell, including which genes are on or off and which are mutated, can change very quickly and radically.

The T cells of our immune system can detect abnormal, potentially dangerous cells, and when they do they order those cells to commit suicide. The gross changes in a cancer cell's genetic structure, however, often knock out its ability to respond to those signals. When this happens, the cancer cell has gained immunity to apoptosis and is well on its way to fulfilling its quest for immortality and assuming the lifestyle enjoyed by its protozoan ancestors.

A Disease of the Genes

It may seem odd that our genes can make us sick, and even kill us, for they are, in a sense, our most trusted ally. Their evolution, stretching back 3.5 billion years, made life what it is today: vigorous, diverse, and perfectly adapted to Earth's many environments. At the cellular level, dozens of enzymes devote themselves to tending the chromosomes and the genes they contain, like worker bees tending their queen. When genes are damaged, the enzymes repair them; when the genes need to divide, the enzymes carefully copy each chromosome into an exact duplicate; and when it is time for the cell to divide, the enzyme attendants move the chromosomes into position, attach them to the spindle, and gently send them on their way.

A gene giving us cancer is like a queen bee stinging a caretaker drone to death. When a tumor forms, some of our genes cross the line from a good gene that codes for an important cellular protein to a bad gene that produces a protein capable of sending us to an early grave. Fortunately for us, the number of cancer-causing genes is small compared with the 30,000 we possess. Genes that cause cancer do so by gaining a new function or by losing their normal function. The gain-of-function cancer genes are called oncogenes, and their normal counterparts are called proto-oncogenes. The loss-of-function cancer genes are called tumor suppressor genes (TSGs), because their normal job is to keep the cell from dividing inappropriately.

Tumor Suppressor Genes

Three genes, called *rb, p53,* and *p21,* code for proteins (RB, P53, and P21) that act as tumor suppressor genes (TSGs), and all of them are required for the G_1 checkpoint to work properly (see table on page 32). The *rb* gene, the first tumor suppressor gene to be identified, was discovered in a study of retinoblastoma, a rare childhood cancer of the eye. Subsequent studies have shown that *rb* codes for a protein that is involved in blocking DNA synthesis when the G_1 checkpoint detects a problem and is expressed in all cells of the body. The function of this gene is now known to be abnormal, or simply lost, in many kinds of cancers, including carcinomas of the lung, breast, and bladder.

The *p53* gene (named after the weight of the gene's protein product) may be the most important cancer-causing gene known, as its loss of function is associated with more than half of all known cancers. This gene, like *rb,* blocks progression through S phase when DNA damage is detected. It does this indirectly by activating the synthesis of P21, which binds to the DNA to block replication. In addition, *p53* mediates external requests (primarily from T cells) for the cell to commit suicide. Consequently, cancer cells lacking a functional *p53* gene can divide without restraint, and they are no longer under the control of the immune system or inhibiting signals from neighboring cells, meaning they are immune to apoptosis.

Tumor suppressor genes (TSGs) lose their normal function as a consequence of a point mutation (a change affecting single nucleotide), leading to a defective protein. The mutation may occur spontaneously, or it may be induced by radiation, such as UV light, X-rays, or radioac-

EXAMPLES OF CANCER GENES

Gene	Type	Function	Tumor
p53	Tumor suppressor	G_1 checkpoint/apoptosis	Carcinoma
rb	Tumor suppressor	G_1 checkpoint	Carcinoma
p21	Tumor suppressor	G_1 checkpoint	Carcinoma
ras	Oncogene	G-protein	Sarcoma
src	Oncogene	Tyrosine kinase	Sarcoma
myc	Oncogene	Transcription factor	Carcinoma

Cancers are caused by loss-of-function tumor suppressor genes (TSGs) and gain-of-function oncogenes. The *p53* gene may be the most important cancer-causing gene of all, as it is associated with half of all known cancers. Oncogenes generally overstimulate signaling pathways that promote cell proliferation, leading to uncontrolled cell division. By convention, gene names are written in italics.

tivity, or by noxious chemicals, such as pesticides, industrial pollutants, or those found in tobacco smoke.

Oncogenes and Proto-oncogenes

An oncogene is produced when its normal counterpart, the proto-oncogene, is altered in some way. Research in many laboratories over the past 20 years has shown that the conversion of proto-oncogenes to oncogenes (a PO conversion) occurs by essentially two methods: a point mutation, occurring as described above for TSGs, and insertional mutagenesis. If the mutation occurs within the gene's promoter (the genetic element that turns a gene on or off), the protein product will be the same before and after the conversion, but the amount of the protein will be different. More commonly, the mutation occurs within the coding region, in which case the protein still functions, but it does its job in a much different way. It is for this reason that oncogenes are referred to as gain-of-function cancer genes. In the second method of PO conversion, insertional mutagenesis, a retrovirus inserts itself into a chromosome as part of its own life cycle.

Oncogenes have names that are derived from the type of cancer they induce or are associated with (see table above). For example, the *ras* (rhymes with "gas") oncogene was originally isolated from a rat sarcoma; *myc* (pronounced "mick") is often expressed in a leukemia called myelocytoma; and *src* (pronounced "sark"), the first oncogene to be discovered, was isolated from a chicken sarcoma. For convenience, onco-

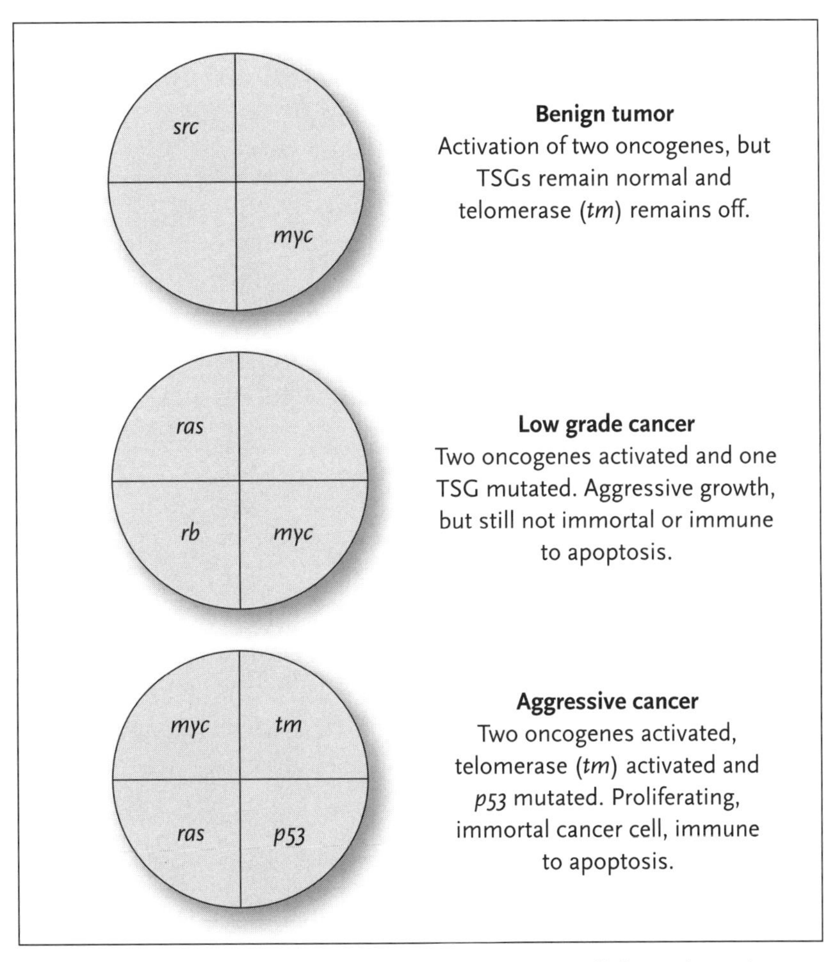

A dangerous mix of genes. The deadliness of a cancer cell depends on the mix of genes it can turn on or off. Activating two oncogenes while telomerase (*tm*) remains off and tumor suppressor genes (TSGs) remain normal leads to cell growth but not immortality or metastasis. Activating two oncogenes and telomerase and mutating *p53* leads to the formation of an aggressive metastatic cancer.

genes and proto-oncogenes have the same name; that is, the *myc* oncogene is also the *myc* proto-oncogene. It is usually clear from the context of the discussion which is being referred to. Many oncogenes, including *ras, myc,* and *src,* stimulate proliferation-signaling pathways, forcing the cell to divide uncontrollably. Oncogenes were discovered in the 1980s by Dr. J. Michael Bishop and Dr. Harold Varmus, for which they shared the 1989 Nobel Prize in medicine.

A Dangerous Mix

A potential cancer cell that activates one or two oncogenes may be able to grow inappropriately, but it will produce only a harmless benign tumor. On the other hand, cancer cells become deadly when they simultaneously activate two oncogenes and telomerase (discussed in chapter 1) and deactivate a tumor suppressor gene.

The issue of cancer induction and treatment becomes very complex when we include all the known and potential cancer-causing genes, which number close to 100. Scientists know that the cell cycle is central to cancer induction and have identified the major components of the G_1 checkpoint, but very little is known about the proteins that manage the G_2 and metaphase checkpoints. Many cancer cells are undoubtedly mutating genes controlling these checkpoints in order to acquire immortality and the power of metastasis.

Nevertheless, real excitement exists in cancer research today, because scientists have finally identified the molecular events that lead to some of the deadliest forms of cancer, such as those affecting the pancreas, liver, and colon. Perhaps for the first time in 20 years, since the war on cancer began, we may feel confident that cures for these terrible diseases are close at hand.

·4· CANCER PROGRESSION

Cancers usually take a long time to develop. This is because, as pointed out in previous chapters, there must be a defect in more than one gene before a cell can make the switch. Potential cancer cells appear continuously throughout an individual's life, but most are destroyed by the immune system, and still others never manage to develop a lethal genetic profile. For a cancer to develop, all the "right" conditions must exist simultaneously in the same cell. This is the reason a tumor appears originally in only one part of the body and, over the years, spreads to other areas.

Cancers Develop from a Single Bad Cell

Cancer cells within a tumor are like any other living community in that they are subject to the same laws of natural selection. Most cancer cells die spontaneously because their genome has been so badly corrupted that they are incapable of maintaining basic housekeeping functions. Of those that survive, one may have a genetic profile that favors rapid growth, so much so that it quickly becomes the only cell type within the tumor. This scenario has been confirmed experimentally by examining characteristics of cancer cells isolated from different regions of a single individual's body. For example, certain forms of leukemia are associated with the presence of the Philadelphia chromosome, created by a translocation between the long arms of chromosomes 9 and 22 (described in chapter 2). Detailed sequence analysis of the DNA spanning the break site shows it is identical in all leukemic cells from a single patient, confirming a common ancestry. In other words, the leukemia cells in that particular patient are all derived from a single cancerous founder cell.

The Switch from Benign to Malignant Tumors

Malignant cancer cells are those that have acquired the ability to leave the tumor of their origin and migrate throughout the body where they initiate the formation of new tumors. This process, called metastasis, requires the following conditions: First, the cancer cell must be able to break away from the tumor mass. Second, once it has broken free, it must be able to migrate throughout the intercellular space until it contacts a blood vessel; at this stage the cancer is locally invasive. Third, the cancer cell must be able to penetrate a blood vessel in order to enter general circulation, which carries the cell to a new location where it forms new tumors. Scientists believe each step in the development of invasiveness and metastasis is controlled by a separate group of genes, but so far no such genes have been identified.

However, it is possible to infer the identities of some of the genes, based on the requirements at each step. Separation of a cancer cell from the rest of the tumor requires the breaking of chemical bonds that normally hold cells together. The most important of these are mediated by cell surface proteins called cadherins, which project from every cell, allowing two or more cells to make physical connections. Disruption of these bonds may occur in cancer cells when the gene coding for a cadherin mutates, thus producing a defective protein. Metastasis, invasiveness, and penetration of blood vessels requires the activation of genes that make it possible for the cell to move, much like an amoeba or a macrophage of the immune system. Since more than 80 percent of all human cancers are carcinomas (cancers of stationary epithelial cells) the acquisition of motility is a crucial step. If it were possible to block this step, all cancers could be reduced to harmless benign tumors. One gene, called *Rho,* shows increased expression in aggressively metastatic cancers, and it is known that this gene is involved in regulating cell motility in protozoans and macrophages. It is hoped that with the completion of the human genome project it will soon be possible to identify other genes involved in metastasis.

The Role of Sex Hormones

Hormones such as estrogen, progesterone, and testosterone prepare the human body for reproduction and stimulate the development of sexual characteristics as an individual passes through puberty. In women, estrogen stimulates development of the breasts, ovaries, uterus, and the general shape of the body. The cells of the uterine lining are stimulated to grow and divide every month as part of the woman's menstrual cycle. If a pregnancy occurs, progesterone, along with estrogen, helps maintain the uterine lining to support development of the fetus. In men, testosterone stimulates development of the testes, sperm production, and growth of facial hair and musculature.

The sex hormones exert their varied effects by promoting cell growth and cell division. As long as the cells in the target organs are healthy, with checkpoint monitors intact, there is no problem. But if a crucial gene or set of genes is defective, and the cell is being bombarded with signals to proliferate, the situation can become serious very quickly. This is the reason why cancers of the breast, uterus, ovaries, and prostate are so common and so dangerous. Cancers such as these are a natural consequence of reproductive physiology, and treatments often try to reduce the levels of sex hormones to withdraw the stimulus to the tumor cells. As discussed more fully in the next chapter, this approach is not a pleasant experience, involving as it often does the removal of the ovaries, to eliminate the synthesis of estrogen, or the testes, to block production of testosterone.

The relationship between steroid hormones and cancer production introduces serious concerns regarding hormone replacement therapy, particularly for women, to minimize bone loss in the elderly. Hormone replacement therapy can alleviate some of the symptoms of osteoporosis in men and women, but it may do so at the risk of developing cancer. Similar concerns exist in the sporting world, where steroids are used to enhance performance. While such treatments seem to be effective, the athlete who uses hormone supplements will likely pay a heavy price for it in later life by developing prostate, breast, or uterine cancer.

Aging and the Incidence of Cancer

Human cancer is primarily an age-related disease that strikes when an individual is 50 years of age or older. The age of the individual and the time element are important largely because the formation of a tumor is a multistep process that takes many years to complete. There are, however, many exceptions to the age-cancer relationship. Lung cancer brought on by cigarette smoke and childhood leukemias are the most notable examples. The chemicals in cigarette smoke are known to accelerate tumor formation, but the factors responsible for cancer acceleration in children are still unclear.

Cancers are age-related because our cells change with time, becoming more susceptible to genetic damage and less capable of dealing with the damage when it does occur. This problem is believed to be due, in large measure, to a reduction in the ability of our immune system to track down and destroy abnormal cells as they appear; the body's diminished immune response gives those cells time to evolve into a potentially lethal cancer.

The increased incidence of cancer in those age 50 and older is also coincidental with the onset of sexual senescence in both men and women. It is quite possible that the hormonal changes that occur during this period contribute to our increased susceptibility to cancer. Age-related hormonal changes are primarily concerned with a shift in the ratio of estrogen to testosterone (ET ratio) in both men and women. Young women have a high estrogen/testosterone ratio (a lot of estrogen, very little testosterone), whereas young men have a low estrogen/testosterone ratio (a lot of testosterone, very little estrogen). Estrogen levels drop dramatically in women after menopause, and men show a similar decline in the level of testosterone at a corresponding age. As a consequence, men and women approach a similar ET ratio between the ages of 50 and 80, which is thought to influence the rate at which genetic instability occurs. In addition, many scientists believe the shift in the ET ratio is largely responsible for the weakening of our immune system, leading to the increased occurrence not only of cancer but of many other diseases as well.

Carcinogens

Many cancers are an unfortunate consequence of our physiology, biochemistry, and cellular ancestry, but an even greater number may be caused by chemicals or radiation in our environment. Cancer-causing agents such as these are called carcinogens. The National Institutes of Health (NIH) in the United States currently lists more than 200 known or suspected carcinogens. Radiation that can cause cancer is usually high doses of ultraviolet (UV) light, X-rays, and various forms of high-energy radiation produced by radioactive materials. The nature of chemical carcinogens is highly variable, ranging from industrial pollutants to the cooking grease used in fast-food restaurants, all of which are suspected of causing cancer. Surprisingly, there is very little evidence to support these suspicions. Of all the suspected cases of cancer induction from industrial sources, only two, asbestos and beta-napthylamine, have been confirmed as carcinogens in epidemiological studies (studies of a disease and the factors affecting its occurrence).

Asbestos is a generic name given to a group of six naturally occurring fibrous silicate minerals. Asbestos minerals possess a number of desirable properties that were useful in commercial applications, including heat stability and thermal and electrical insulation. Although asbestos use dates back at least 2,000 years, modern industrial use began in about 1880, reaching a peak in the late 1960s and early 1970s when more than 3,000 industrial applications or products were listed. This material has been used primarily in roofing, production of plastics, and thermal and electrical insulation.

Beta-naphthylamine, also known as 2-naphthylamine, occurs as colorless or white-to-reddish crystals with a faint aromatic odor that darken in air to a purple-red color. It is soluble in hot water, alcohol, ether, and many organic solvents. This compound is currently used for research purposes only, but in the mid-1950s it was used as an intermediate in the manufacture of dyes and as an antioxidant in the production of rubber for automobile tires, among other uses.

Asbestos is now known to cause lung cancer, and beta-naphthylamine, in one prominent case, was shown to cause bladder cancer in virtually all of the British factory workers who were exposed to it in the 1950s. However, the number of people dying because of these carcinogens is no greater than the millions of deaths attributable to aflatoxin, a naturally occurring compound produced by the common bread mold *Aspergillus oryzae.* This fungus grows on grains and peanuts when they are stored under humid tropical conditions, and the aflatoxin it produces is thought to be the cause of liver cancer in the tropics.

However, the deadliest carcinogens by far are found in cigarette smoke, and among the 40 or so that have been identified, the best

DNA adducts. Normal DNA is free of adducts. Carcinogens can bind directly to the DNA, forming a carcinogen-nucleotide base complex known as adducts. The adducts can interfere with the accuracy of replication, thus accelerating the mutation rate. The adducts shown here are formed by benzopyrene (black circles), a compound that binds to guanine (G).

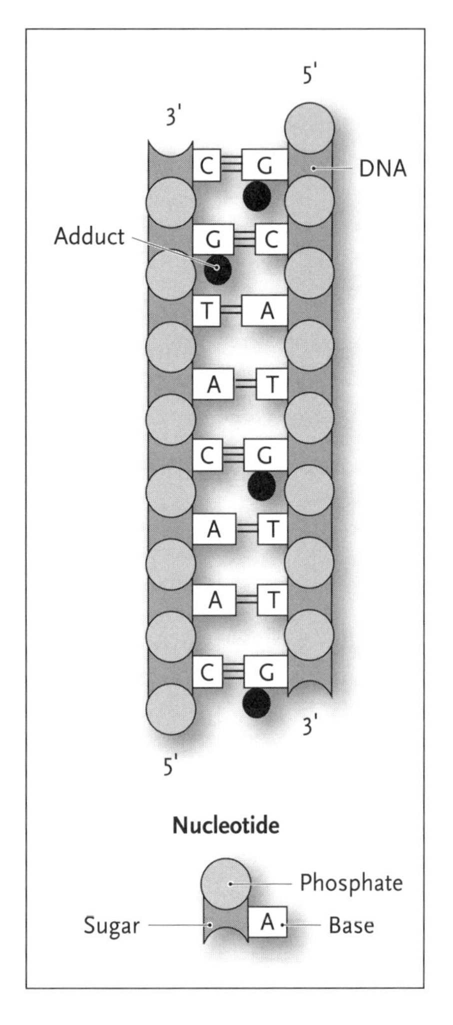

studied is a compound called benzopyrene. This molecule, when intact, is not dangerous, but when a cigarette is smoked the benzopyrene enters the blood and travels to the liver where it is inadvertently activated. An important function of our liver is to detoxify our blood by breaking down a wide variety of compounds, from alcohol to aspirin. A special set of liver enzymes, called mixed-function oxidases, breaks the alcohol down and either stores or eliminates the pieces. In the case of benzopyrene, the oxidases activate the molecule in such a way that it gains the ability to bind to guanine, thus forming DNA adducts.

The binding of benzopyrene to DNA is not a problem in itself, as long as the cell is postmitotic. However, DNA adducts greatly increase the error frequency associated with DNA replication. Cells in the lung are not postmitotic but divide frequently, and if those cells contain DNA adducts, errors will be introduced into their genome with each round of the cell cycle. Making the situation even worse, other ingredients in tobacco smoke stimulate proliferation-signaling pathways, much as certain oncogenes do, forcing the cells to divide more frequently than normal. The carcinogens' combined ability to form DNA adducts and to force a cell to divide when it should not accelerates the mutation rate and onset of cancers. An accelerated mutation rate increases the risk of damaging a tumor suppressor gene or of activating an oncogene. These changes set the stage for serious trouble to come.

Lung cancer and other cancers caused by tobacco smoke kill more than 400,000 men and women every year in the United States alone and account for nearly 30 percent of annual U.S. cancer deaths. Smokers are 20 times more likely to die of cancer than nonsmokers. Worldwide, 4 million people die every year of cancers caused by tobacco smoke. In China, where two-thirds of the adult male population smokes tobacco, close to 1 million die each year of tobacco-related cancers. Lung cancer alone is so prevalent that it has obscured the incidence of all other cancers. Many people have the impression that the incidence of cancer cases has been increasing over the years, and if all cancers are simply grouped together and plotted against time, this does appear to be the case. Many believe the increased prevalence of cancer is due to pollution of our environment, the air we breathe, and the food we eat. Yet if lung cancer is subtracted from the data, we find that the incidence of other major cancers (plotted as deaths per 100,000 people), including colon, breast, and prostate cancer, has not changed since 1930.

It is quite possible that the elimination of tobacco carcinogens would lower the rates for other cancers as well, since it is likely that compounds such as benzopyrene are contributing to the onset of cancers in other organs of the body. Not surprisingly, smoking tobacco is associated with an increased risk for cancers of the mouth, throat, stomach, pancreas (the deadliest of all cancers), liver, uterus, kidney, and bladder. It may also be responsible for the increased prevalence of leukemia in adults and children, the latter presumably caused by secondary smoke inhalation. Indeed, laboratory rats and mice forced to smoke the equivalent of a pack of cigarettes a day develop benzopyrene DNA adducts in virtually every tissue of the body. If we are ever able to remove tobacco carcinogens from our daily lives, it may well turn out that cancer is more a consequence of *our* lifestyle, rather than that of our protozoan ancestors.

·5·

CANCER THERAPIES

The versatility, adaptability, and extreme cleverness of cancer cells have made it very difficult for scientists to develop methods to either contain or eradicate this disease. Treatment is complicated by the exact nature of the cancer cells, the tissue they arose from, and the tissue or tissues they end up colonizing. Many cancers, such as those affecting the colon or liver, remain tucked away in the darker recesses of the body, where they are hard to detect and even harder to treat. Other cancers, such as melanoma or retinoblastoma, are at or near the surface of the body, and thus are more accessible to observation and treatment. All cancer therapies try to target characteristics that are peculiar to cancer cells so as not to damage normal cells. This could be a mutated protein, a peculiar behavior pattern, such as an increased rate of cell division, or an elevated demand for oxygen to support the cancer cell's high metabolic activity.

Angiogenesis Blockers

All cells, whether they are cancerous or not, need to be vascularized in order to receive the oxygen and nutrients required to support metabolic activity. Blood vessels also carry away metabolic waste products, such as carbon dioxide, which is expelled from the body by the lungs, and urea, expelled by the kidneys. The circulatory system, consisting of an extensive collection of arteries, veins, and capillaries, provides these essential services. Installing this system requires the formation of new blood vessels, a process that is called angiogenesis.

Angiogenesis is, of course, extremely important during embryogenesis, when the circulatory system is being formed, and during growth to adulthood. Vascularization during development is so efficient that virtually every cell in the body is less than 100 μm away from the nearest capillary. Angiogenesis also has many important roles to play during adulthood, such as wound healing, formation of the corpus luteum after ovulation, formation of new endometrium after menstruation, and remodeling the vasculature of skeletal muscle after long periods of exercise.

There are many factors involved in the formation of blood vessels, but the best understood are a tyrosine kinase called vascular endothelial growth factor (VEGF) and a gene regulatory protein called hypoxia-inducible factor 1 (HIF-1). A shortage of oxygen in any cell of the body activates HIF-1, which, in turn, stimulates production and secretion of VEGF. The VEGF protein induces proliferation of endothelial cells (cells that make up blood vessels) that sprout from the nearest capillary and, following the VEGF concentration gradient, grow towards the hypoxic cells. Once the cells are vascularized and begin receiving an adequate oxygen supply, HIF-1 is inactivated and production of VEGF drops off, thus terminating angiogenesis.

Tumors, like normal tissue, cannot grow to more than a millimeter or two in diameter without being vascularized. Consequently, angiogenesis is a prime target for cancer therapy. Clinical trials are currently in progress to test angiogenesis inhibitors on cancers of the breast, prostate, brain, pancreas, lung, stomach, ovary, and cervix, as well as leukemia and lymphomas. So far the studies have had limited success. Endostatin, a widely studied drug that is toxic to endothelial cells, showed great promise in preliminary studies. It is safe to administer, but it has failed to demonstrate antitumor effects. An extract from the Asian fruit *Gleditsia sinensis* (GSE) has been shown to be an effective blocker of VEGF transcription but has yet to progress beyond the basic research stage. Another compound, extracted from green tea, called GTE is known to be a powerful blocker of endothelial cell proliferation but, like GSE, it is still at the preclinical stage of development. The most successful angiogenesis blocker tested so far is an anti-VEGF antibody called bevacizumab. This drug is being tested in phase I clinical trials, but it will be several years before this drug or any of the other known angiogenesis blockers are approved for routine medical use.

Biotherapies

Cancer therapies that exploit the body's immune system are known as biotherapies or immunotherapies. The use of an antibody to deactivate VEGF is an example of a biotherapy. Biotherapy exploits the properties of the adaptive immune system, which involves the white blood cells (WBCs) called T lymphocytes and B lymphocytes. B lymphocytes produce antibodies tailored for microbe antigens. T lymphocytes, or T cells, are activated by other white blood cells, called monocytes, in a way that alerts the T cell to specific invader antigens. The T cell uses this information to hunt down and destroy those invaders. T cells enlist the aid of other lymphocytes by secreting small signaling molecules called cytokines. A special kind of T cell, called a natural killer (NK) lymphocyte, is activated by the release of cytokines but focuses its attention on attacking and killing infected cells rather than the invading microbe (see chapter 8 for additional information). The immune system also attacks cancer cells because they usually contain mutated proteins, displayed on the cell surface, that are treated as being of foreign origin. Biotherapies exploit the strategies of the immune system by employing cytokines, bone marrow stimulants, and monoclonal antibodies.

CYTOKINES The first successful biotherapy came with the isolation of a cytokine known as interferon, which stimulates NK cells and seems to have a direct effect on some cancer cells by slowing their growth rate and stimulating more normal behavior. The U.S. Food and Drug Administration (FDA) has approved the use of interferon to treat kidney cancers, lymphoma, and Kaposi's sarcoma. Other cytokines, called interleukins, have been used to specifically boost the response of T lymphocytes. There are more than 30 known interleukins, but the most promising so far is interleukin-2 (IL-2), which has been approved for the treatment of kidney carcinomas and melanoma. In addition, clinical trials are under way to test the effectiveness of IL-2 as a treatment for cancers of the colon, ovaries, lung, brain, breast, prostate, and bone marrow (leukemia).

BONE MARROW STIMULANTS Biological therapies sometimes take a more generalized approach to treating cancer. One such effort involves the use of colony-stimulating factor (CSF) to stimulate cell growth in the bone marrow. Its presence increases the number of WBCs, thus augmenting the immune response, but it also increases the number of red blood cells (RBCs) to improve the overall health and vitality of the patient. RBCs contain the oxygen-carrying pigment hemoglobin and have the very important job of delivering oxygen to all of the cells. Thus, CSF helps ensure that all cells are receiving an adequate supply of oxygen and that the patient does not become anemic. This is an important consideration since the patient may also be receiving chemotherapy or radiotherapy, both of which can damage the bone marrow, leading to an increased incidence of secondary infections and anemia. Administration of CSF can help counteract this effect and, indeed, makes it possible for a patient to tolerate levels of chemotherapy or radiotherapy that would not be possible otherwise.

MONOCLONAL ANTIBODIES The final form of biotherapy, currently being practiced, involves the use of monoclonal antibodies (MAbs). A single type of B cell, grown in culture, produces these antibodies, which are specific for a single antigen. All the cells in the culture originate from a single founder cell that produces the desired antibody. The cells are thus clones of the original cell, so the antibody they make is said to be monoclonal. MAbs are produced by injecting a single kind of human cancer cell into mice to stimulate the production of antibodies. The mouse cells producing the antibodies are isolated and fused with a culture of immortalized human cells to produce a hybridoma. The hybridomas are also an immortalized cell line, and thus can produce a very large quantity of the antibody. Production of MAbs maximizes the specificity of the antibody to ensure that it will not react with or damage antigens on normal cells. MAbs can be designed to attack cancer cells directly, or they can be linked to cytotoxic substances that destroy the cancer cell after it encounters the MAb.

Rituxin and Herceptin are two MAbs that have been approved by the FDA as cancer treatments. Rituxin is used to treat Hodgkin's lymphoma, and Herceptin is used to treat breast cancer. Clinical trials are under way to test a large number of MAbs for the treatment of cancers described in chapter 1.

Bone Marrow Transplants

Transplanting bone marrow (BM) is a common method for treating leukemia and lymphoma. It is also required when radiotherapy is used to treat other forms of cancer, because this therapy often destroys or damages the patient's bone marrow. There are three types of BM transplants, each defined in terms of the donor tissue: autogeneic transplants, in which patients receive their own BM; syngeneic transplants, in which patients receive BM from an identical twin; and allogeneic transplants, in which patients receive BM from unrelated individuals. Autogeneic transplants are most commonly used when chemotherapy or radiotherapy has damaged the patient's bone marrow. Patients suffering from leukemia or lymphoma generally receive syngeneic or allogeneic transplants. Syngeneic transplants are preferred, in order to avoid immune rejection. However, very few patients have identical twins; consequently, the great majority of BM transplants are allogeneic. Allogeneic transplants will be attacked by the immune system, giving rise to a condition known as graft-versus-host disease (GVHD), making it necessary for these patients to take immunosuppressant drugs for the remainder of their lives.

The immune system's decision to accept or reject a given tissue is based on the exact nature of the glycocalyx, the molecular forest covering the surface of each cell in the grafted tissue. The glycocalyx consists of millions of different kinds of glycoproteins that protrude from the cell surface. Immunologists call these glycoproteins cell-surface antigens. Members of the immune system, particularly T lymphocytes, can tell if a cell is foreign or not by examining these glycoproteins. Immunologists have identified many of these glycoproteins and use this information to match donated BM to prospective patients. Given that there are so many different kinds of antigens it may seem like an impossible task. However, some glycoproteins seem to be more important than others, when it comes to invoking GVHD, so immunologists have obtained good results by matching just five or six strong antigens (see chapter 8 for details). Matching BM for a few antigens still leaves many that are unmatched, and consequently the grafted tissue will be rejected over time. However, a partial match can still reduce the amount of immunosuppressants the patient must take over a lifetime while improving the long-term survival of the transplanted tissue.

Chemotherapy

Certain drugs may be used to kill or inhibit the growth of cancer cells. The nature of a drug varies depending on the type of cancer, its location in the body, the effect it has on normal body functions, and the overall health of the patient. In general, cancer drugs damage DNA, block the synthesis of DNA and RNA, or damage the mitotic spindle. Cancer drugs can also interfere with normal physiology by blocking steroid hormone receptors that stimulate cancer cell growth.

DRUGS THAT TARGET DNA These agents chemically damage DNA and RNA, leading to a disruption of replication (DNA synthesis) or transcription (RNA synthesis). In some cases these drugs lead to the production of defective messenger RNA that is incapable of coding for protein. Examples of this type of drug are cisplatin, doxorubicin, and etoposide.

DRUGS THAT BLOCK DNA AND RNA SYNTHESIS These drugs work by blocking the formation of ribonucleotides or deoxyribonucleotides, essential building blocks for RNA and DNA. Without nucleotides, the cell cannot replicate, cannot repair its DNA, and is incapable of synthesizing new proteins. Examples of these drugs are methotrexate, mercaptopurine, and fluorouracil.

DRUGS THAT DAMAGE THE MITOTIC SPINDLE The mitotic spindle is a collection of microtubules that serve to carry the chromosomes to opposite poles of a dividing cell. Disruption of the spindle is an effective way of blocking cell division. Drugs in this class include Vinblastine, Vincristine, and Taxol.

DRUGS THAT BLOCK HORMONE RECEPTORS Breast cancer may be caused by the lifelong exposure of breast cells to the growth-stimulating effects of the female steroid hormone, estrogen. Under normal circumstances, the effects of estrogen are essential for the growth of breast cells leading to the production of milk after a woman gives birth. However, if a tumor appears in the breast, a reasonable strategy is to neutralize the stimulatory effects of estrogen, in the hope that it will arrest the growth of the cancer. A plant extract called tamoxifen has been shown to be an estrogen antagonist; that is, it binds to the estrogen receptor, thus blocking the hormone's normal functions. For men, counterpart to this strategy involves the use of antiandrogen drugs, specifically to block testosterone receptors, to treat prostate cancer. A drug used for this purpose is called bicalutamide.

Chemotherapy may be administered daily, weekly, or monthly but generally occurs in cycles that include long rest periods, giving the body a chance to recover. Normally the drugs are administered intravenously (IV) although some may be taken as a pill or, in the case of surface cancers such as melanoma, applied directly to the skin. Patients requiring many IV treatments are fitted with a catheter, a soft flexible tube that is inserted into a large vein, thus avoiding the necessity of daily injections.

Drugs used in chemotherapy are designed to target cancer cells, but they often damage or kill normal cells as well. Death of normal cells leads to a variety of side effects, some of them quite severe. Cancer drugs target actively dividing cells; consequently, any normal tissue consisting of proliferating cells will also be affected, most notably the bone marrow, digestive tract, testes, ovaries, and hair follicles. Some drugs may also affect postmitotic cells in the heart, kidney, bladder, lungs, and nervous system. In some cases, these tissues may be permanently damaged. Given the range of tissues affected, it is not surprising that chemotherapy involving the first three categories described above is associated with a large number of side effects: fatigue, nausea and vomiting, pain, hair loss, anemia, secondary infections, and poor blood clotting.

FATIGUE Feeling tired, with a complete lack of energy, is the most common symptom reported by cancer patients. This is partly due to the stress of hospitalization and the lack of sleep this may entail, but it is mainly the result of low blood counts and poor appetite brought on by the cancer drugs.

NAUSEA AND VOMITING This side effect is due almost entirely to the death of epithelial cells lining the digestive tract. These are actively dividing cells that are very sensitive to chemotherapy. Anticancer drugs are designed to minimize this side effect, but residual discomfort may be minimized with antinausea treatments.

PAIN Chemotherapy sometimes damages neurons in the peripheral nervous system, leading to burning, numbness, and tingling or shooting pain, usually in the finger or toes. Some cancer drugs can also cause mouth sores, headaches, muscle pain, and stomach pain associated with nausea and vomiting. These pains are usually no more severe than those accompanying a flu, and are treated with common painkillers such as aspirin or acetaminophen.

HAIR LOSS Hair follicles, like intestinal epithelium, are actively dividing cells that are killed by chemotherapy. The death of these cells is responsible for the loss of hair, not only on the head, but also over the entire body. The hair grows back when chemotherapy is discontinued, but sometimes the new hair is a different color, or it has a different texture.

ANEMIA Chemotherapy greatly reduces the bone marrow's ability to make red blood cells (RBCs); consequently, the amount of oxygen reaching the cells is reduced. A decrease in the RBC count leads to a condition known as anemia, the symptoms of which include shortness of breath, dizziness, and a feeling of being tired and weak. In severe cases, anemia can be treated with a blood transfusion, or with a growth factor called erythropoietin that stimulates the formation of RBCs.

INFECTION In addition to reducing production of RBCs, chemotherapy also reduces the production of white blood cells (WBCs), the cells of the immune system. Consequently, the patient becomes more susceptible to infections and must take precautions, such as staying away from people who have a cold or flu, and avoiding sharp objects that might cut the skin, such as sewing needles and razors. Treating the patient with colony-stimulating factor, a type of hormone that promotes the growth and differentiation of white blood cells, offsets the reduction in the WBC count.

BLOOD CLOTTING PROBLEMS In addition to RBC and WBC, the bone marrow produces a third kind of blood cell, called platelets, which are needed for the blood to clot properly. In the absence of external cuts, low platelet counts can lead to excessive bruising, red spots under the skin, blood in the urine, bleeding nose and gums, and headaches.

Cryosurgery

Freezing cancer cells or tumors with liquid nitrogen (–196°C) is called cryosurgery. For external tumors of the skin, liquid nitrogen is applied with a very fine spray gun. For internal locations, surgeons use an instrument called a cryoprobe that is placed in contact with the tumor. Ultrasound imaging is sometimes used to monitor the placement of the probe and freezing of the tissue. The treatment generally involves three freeze-thaw cycles to ensure destruction of the cancer cells.

Cryosurgery is used to treat skin, prostate, lung, and cervical cancers. Research is in progress to test the effectiveness of this treatment on other types of cancers, such as cancers of bone, brain, spine, and windpipe. This procedure offers several advantages over other forms of treatment. It is less invasive than ordinary surgery, requiring only a small incision in the skin for insertion of the cryoprobe and imaging tube. Treatment is highly localized, with minimal damage to surrounding tissue, and can be repeated many times. The main disadvantage of this procedure is that it can be used only on tumors confined to a small area. In addition, cancer cells that have separated from the main tumor mass will be missed. Consequently, cryosurgery is often used in conjunction with chemotherapy or radiotherapy.

Cryosurgery does have some side effects, but they are much less severe than those associated with other forms of therapy. Used on liver cancers, the procedure will sometimes damage the bile ducts or major blood vessels, leading to hemorrhage (extensive bleeding) or infection. Cryosurgery of the prostate gland can damage the urinary tract and local nerves, leading to sexual impotence and incontinence (lack of control over urine flow), although these side effects are often temporary.

Gene Therapy

Since cancer is a disease of the genes it can, in theory, be treated by either repairing the defective gene or by introducing a normal copy of the gene into the affected tissue. This procedure, known as gene therapy, was pioneered in the 1990s to treat genetic deficiencies of the immune system. Since that time, more than 600 gene therapy trials have been launched in the United States alone, of which 60 percent are designed to treat various types of cancer.

Introducing a gene into a cell is a complex and often dangerous business that depends on the natural ability of viruses to infect cells. Some RNA viruses, called retroviruses, have the added ability to incorporate their genome into cellular chromosomes. Scientists have developed methods for adding a human gene to the retroviral genome, so that when the retrovirus infects a cell and inserts its genome into a chromosome, it has, in effect, delivered and installed the therapeutic gene. To be sure, there are many wrinkles in this procedure, and much work is needed to ensure the virus does not damage the cell or the patient, and that the therapeutic gene is expressed at levels sufficient to cure the cancer (see chapter 8 for a gene therapy primer).

Most of the gene therapy trials aimed at treating cancer introduce a normal copy of the tumor suppressor gene *p53*. As described in chapter 3, *p53* codes for a protein (P53) that blocks cell division in abnormal cells and can, if necessary, force defective cells to commit suicide. The *p53* gene is abnormal in more than half of all cancers and is thus a prime target for therapy. Currently, *p53*-gene therapy clinical trials are under way to treat cancers of the ovaries, breast, prostate, head and neck, liver and bone marrow (leukemia). Other genes, specific for breast cancer (BRCA1 and BRCA2), melanoma (CDKN2, or cyclin-dependent kinase N2), and colon cancer (MSH1 and MSH2) are also the subject of gene therapy trials.

Side effects associated with gene therapy are invariably due either to immune attack on the cells that become infected with the vector (the virus carrying the therapeutic gene) or to complications resulting from insertional mutagenesis, whereby the vector damages a cellular gene when it inserts itself into a chromosome. In the former case, the immune response can be so extreme as to lead to multiorgan failure and subsequent death of the patient. In the latter case, insertional mutagenesis can produce additional cancers.

Laser Therapy

Some cancers may be treated with high-intensity light—a laser—that shrinks or destroys localized tumors. This treatment is often required to treat cancers that are resistant to chemotherapy or radiotherapy. Three types of lasers are currently in use: carbon dioxide (CO_2), neodymium aluminum garnet (NAG), and argon. The CO_2 laser, being of medium intensity, is best suited for treating skin cancers and other superficial tumors. The NAG laser is of high intensity and can penetrate deeper into tissue than light from other lasers can. The light can be carried through optical fibers to organs and tissue deep within the body. The argon laser has the lowest intensity and is used to treat the most superficial skin lesions. It is also used in photodynamic therapy (described below).

CO_2 and NAG lasers are used routinely to treat cancers of the vocal cords, skin, lung, vagina, and colon. The side effects associated with this form of cancer therapy are the same as those for cryosurgery.

Photodynamic Therapy

Treatment using the argon laser, in conjunction with photosensitizing agents to destroy cancer cells and tumors, is called photodynamic therapy. The photosensitizing agent is injected into the bloodstream and absorbed by cells throughout the body. The agents are designed to remain in cancer cells longer than in normal cells. When the treated cancer cells are exposed to the argon laser light, the agent absorbs the light energy, causing it to release oxygen-free radicals that kill the cells. The timing of the therapy is important. It must be given after the agent has left normal cells but when it is still present in cancer cells. In 1998 the FDA approved the use of an agent called porfimer sodium (Photofrin) for the treatment of lung cancer. Several clinical trials are also under way to test the effectiveness of Photofrin on cancers of the bladder, brain, larynx, and oral cavity.

The side effects associated with this therapy can be severe. Photofrin makes the skin and eyes sensitive to light for six weeks or more after treatment. Patients have to avoid sunlight and bright indoor light. Moderate exposure to daylight can result in red, swollen and blistered skin. Other temporary side effects include coughing, difficulty swallowing, abdominal pain, painful breathing and shortness of breath. Photodynamic therapy was invented by Dr. Julia Levi, professor of microbiology at the University of British Columbia.

Radiotherapy

The use of ionizing radiation to destroy cancer cells and tumors is known as radiation therapy, X-ray therapy, irradiation, or simply radiotherapy. This therapy relies on high-energy electromagnetic beams or subatomic particles to damage the DNA in cancer cells so that the cell is incapable of dividing and quickly dies. The main goal is to kill the cancer cells while leaving the normal cells intact. This can be achieved in some cases by focusing the beam of radiation on specific parts of the body or, if possible, directly on the cancerous tumor. Thus radiotherapy has the potential for greater precision than chemotherapy and produces fewer side effects.

Most patients receive external radiotherapy, in which a machine directs the high-energy radiation at the site of the tumor. The most common type of radiation machine is called a linear accelerator. This machine heats a radioactive substance, such as cobalt-60, causing it to liberate high-energy rays. Accelerators can produce X-rays and gamma rays (from cobalt), as well as protons and neutrons. Internal radiotherapy is also possible, in which a radioactive material is sealed inside a holder that is implanted near or within a tumor. This procedure is sometimes used after a tumor has been removed surgically. The implant is placed in the tumor bed (the area previously occupied by the tumor) to kill any residual cancer cells.

For most types of cancer, radiotherapy is given five days a week for six or seven weeks. The total dose of radiation depends on the size of the tumor, but normally, to minimize damage to surrounding tissue many small doses of daily radiation are preferred to fewer larger doses. This strategy is augmented by the recent development of computer-based radiotherapy, which allows precise mapping of the tumor and surrounding tissue so that multiple beams can be shaped to the contour of the treatment area. This type of radiotherapy is used extensively to treat prostate cancer, lung cancer, and certain brain tumors. Radiotherapy is also used to treat cancers of the skin, tongue, breast, uterus and bone marrow. Side effects are as broad as those described for chemotherapy, although less severe.

Stem Cell Therapy

Stem cells are progenitor cells, capable of differentiating into many different cell types that reside in various parts of the body. These cells are used to restore bone marrow in patients who have received chemotherapy, or radiotherapy, for a variety of cancers, but are most commonly used to treat leukemia and lymphomas. In the latter case, the patient's cancerous bone marrow or lymph glands are destroyed with radiotherapy and then reconstituted using stem cells.

Stem cell therapy is similar to the use of bone marrow transplants but has three major advantages: First, the cells are easily isolated from peripheral blood or from umbilical cord blood; second, stem cells are less likely to invoke graft-versus-host disease (GVHD), particularly those from umbilical cord blood, thus most patients do not require immunosuppressants; third, because of reduced risk of GVHD, the donor tissue can be allogeneic and there is no need for tissue matching.

The patient receives the stem cells through a venous catheter placed in a large vein in the neck or chest area. The cells travel to the bone marrow, where they produce new white blood cells, red blood cells, and platelets in a process called engraftment. Reconstitution of the bone marrow takes several weeks, although full recovery of the immune system can take a year or more. The most severe side effect associated with this therapy is the risk of serious infections developing during the period of bone marrow reconstitution. Other side effects such as nausea, vomiting, and hair loss are due to the radiotherapy.

.6.

CANCER AROUND THE WORLD

Cancer has become one of the most devastating diseases worldwide. Every year, 10 million people are diagnosed with cancer, and of these, 6 million will die of this disease. Virtually every family, in every country of the world, has at least one member afflicted with this disease. The disease burden is immense, not only for the victims and their families, but for the medical establishments that struggle to meet the demand for care and treatment.

In 1948 the United Nations established the World Health Organization (WHO) to help people around the world attain the highest level of health. As part of the fight against cancer, WHO has collected data on the worldwide incidence of cancer to give governing bodies an estimate of the magnitude of the problem. This information has provided crucial insights into the causes of cancer and possibilities for treatment and prevention.

The Magnitude of the Problem

Although there are more than 100 different forms of cancer, more than 80 percent of cases involve just 14 types of cancers. WHO has collected detailed information on each of these cancers for nearly every country in the world, most of which are shown in the table on page 56. Africa and South America are the only major regions of the world that record fewer than 1 million cases each year, while North America, Europe, and Asia have between 1 million and 3 million cases each year. When other

THE ANNUAL NUMBER OF NEW CANCER CASES WORLDWIDE

Cancer	Location				
	North America	South America	Europe	Africa	Asia
Bladder	61,875	14,898	136,276	26,048	58,885
Brain	20,251	12,975	49,747	4,852	82,864
Breast	202,044	69,924	346,118	59,167	348,338
Colon	164,673	41,946	362,710	23,454	338,832
Kidney	36,125	10,917	81,130	7,257	50,100
Leukemia	31,706	16,120	65,923	16,046	118,565
Liver	12,535	11,707	49,895	41,788	446,246
Lung	205,608	44,149	375,390	19,476	576,466
Ovaries	23,803	11,603	60,916	12,472	78,973
Pancreas	33,467	12,924	74,249	6,188	83,753
Prostate	211,950	34,286	189,766	27,357	62,313
Skin	43,973	7,321	59,442	8,436	11,187
Stomach	25,585	47,084	192,432	27,953	567,908
Testes	6,588	4,032	23,801	1,587	12,137
Total	**1,080,183**	**339,886**	**2,046,374**	**282,081**	**2,836,567**

Data were compiled from information provided by the World Health Organization and the International Agency for Research on Cancer for 2002. The total number of cancer cases for all areas shown is 6,585,091. When data is added for additional cancers and locations such as Australia and New Zealand, the total number of new cancer cases in 2002 exceeded 10 million.

regions of the world are included, such as the Philippines, Australia, and New Zealand, the combined total exceeds 10 million new cancer cases worldwide each year. The relatively low number of cases recorded in Africa and South America is partly due to inadequate diagnostic facilities, but it also reflects a real regional variation in cancer incidence.

The magnitude of the cancer epidemic defies the medical capabilities of most places in the world. Treatment in North America alone exceeds $1 billion each year, and for the millions of cancer patients who live in poorer countries, the treatments are unavailable or too expensive for the local population to afford. Wealthier countries can better afford cancer treatment; this is fortunate for them, since the highest incidence of nearly all cancers occurs in developed countries.

Developed Countries Have the Highest Cancer Rates

Of the 14 cancers shown in the table on page 56, all but two occur with a higher incidence in developed countries (located in North America, Europe, and parts of Asia). The difference is often profound (see table on page 58). Prostate cancer, at the top of the list, is nearly six times more prevalent in developed companies than it is in undeveloped or less developed countries of the world (located in South America, Africa, and large parts of Asia). Skin cancer, specifically melanoma, is seven times more prevalent in developed countries, while the remaining cancers, shown in the table, are two to three times more prevalent in developed countries. There are two exceptions to this trend: stomach cancer, which occurs with about the same incidence in developed and undeveloped countries, and liver cancer, which is more common in undeveloped countries. The equalized incidence of stomach cancer may point to the ingestion of environmental carcinogens that are present throughout the world (this possibility will be discussed in a later section). The elevated incidence of liver cancer in less developed countries is likely due to the storage of grains in equatorial countries, which promotes the growth of a powerful fungal toxin that is known to cause liver cancer (described in chapter 4).

The data shown in the table on page 56 are averages, and thus they tend to obscure some of the more dramatic differences in cancer

THE INCIDENCE OF COMMON CANCERS IN DEVELOPED AND UNDEVELOPED COUNTRIES

Cancer	Developed Countries*	Undeveloped Countries*
Breast	63	23
Lung	56	25
Prostate	47	8
Colon	37	10
Stomach	25	20
Bladder	19	6
Skin	7	1
Liver	9	17
Kidney	10	2
Leukemia	8	4
Ovary	10	5
Pancreas	8	3
Brain	6	3
Testes	5	1

*Incidence is the number of cases per year, per 100,000 population, adjusted for age, thus eliminating effects of population size and age distribution. Table values are rounded to the nearest whole number. Cancers for breast and ovary are for women; other figures are for men. Data was complied from information provided by the World Health Organization and the International Agency for Research on Cancer for 2002.

prevalence throughout the world. Individual comparisons between specific locations, show a striking trend for each type of cancer (see table on page 59). Again, cancers tend to be more prevalent in developed countries, but in a specific comparison the magnitude of the difference is staggering. The incidence of prostate cancer in the United States is more than 60 times greater than it is in China. Liver cancer in Mongolia is almost 40 times more prevalent than is in Northern Europe, and stomach cancer in Japan is 12 times more common than it is in Africa. These differences are not due to genetic predispositions or resistance to cancers. Chinese people who move to the United States develop prostate cancer at a rate typical for the location. Similarly, West Africans develop colon cancer at a higher rate when they move to North America. Scientists interpret the worldwide variation in cancer rates as an indication that most cancers are caused by diet and lifestyle, and are therefore avoidable.

Cancer and the North American Diet

According to the U.S. Centers for Disease Control (CDC), 64 percent of Americans are overweight. The typical American diet is high in fat and calories, with insufficient quantities of whole grains, fresh fruits, and vegetables. Whole grain breads and cereals, along with fresh fruit and vegetables, are known to reduce the risk of cancer development, particularly colon cancer. The issue of high- versus low-fat diets has traditionally focused on improving an individual's resistance to cardiovascular disease and diabetes. But it has recently become clear that a high-fat diet is directly responsible for the high incidence of many cancers in the developed countries.

Fat has been thought of as a harmless substance, intended for the storage of energy, and historically, this has been the case. When human society was based on hunting and gathering there were periods of the year when individuals would deposit fat as a reserve for the winter months. During other periods of the year, when food was plentiful, the fat reserves were depleted and the individual's physique became slimmer. Women, during their reproductive years, store fat in preparation for childbirth, but again this deposit was transitory, so that men and women cycled between robust and lean physiques. However, in recent times, there has been a clear trend toward the deposition of permanent

THE INCIDENCE OF COMMON CANCERS WORLDWIDE

	High Incidence		Low Incidence	
Cancer	**Location**	**Incidence***	**Location**	**Incidence***
Prostate	United States	104	China	1.7
Liver	Mongolia	99	Northern Europe	2.6
Breast	United States	91	Iran	14.8
Lung	Hong Kong	75	Iran	5.7
Stomach	Japan	69	North Africa	5.6
Colon	North America	55	West Africa	4.3
Bladder	Egypt	45	India	3.2
Skin	Australia	40	China	0.2
Ovary	Denmark	16	North Africa	3.2
Kidney	Germany	13	South-Central Asia	1.2
Brain	Sweden	11	South-Central Asia	2.4
Leukemia	Canada	10	Iran	1.7
Pancreas	Japan	10	India	1.4
Testes	Denmark	10	China	0.4

*Incidence is the number of cases per year, per 100,000 population, adjusted for age, thus eliminating effects of population size and age distribution. Cancers for breast and ovary are for women; other figures are for men. Data were compiled from information provided by the World Health Organization and the International Agency for Research on Cancer for 2002.

body fat, and research has shown a direct link between increased cancer rates and obesity.

Adipocytes, the cells that store fat, increase or decrease in number, depending on the amount of fat being consumed and used. The fat in high-fat diets cannot be metabolized at the rate that it is being ingested, and yet the digestive system is programmed to absorb as much as it can. Consequently, the unused portion is stored in adipocytes, which are capable of proliferating to meet the demand. In other words, development of obesity involves storage of fat and an increase in the number of fat-storing cells. Adipocytes were first identified around the turn of the 20th century, and for more than 90 years these cells were thought of as simple fat-storage depots. This perception changed dramatically in

1995, when several research groups in the United States and Europe discovered that adipocytes synthesize and secrete several growth factors, one of which is called leptin. Leptin has since been shown to be a potent growth factor, capable of stimulating the proliferation of many kinds of cells, including those of the pancreas, liver, lung, stomach, skin, and mammary glands. Even more remarkable is the observation that leptin stimulates the synthesis and secretion of estrogens by adipocytes and by other cells throughout the body, particularly in the ovaries and testes.

The realization that fat cells have an endocrine function came as a surprise to physiologists and endocrinologists. Normally, hormone production is regulated by an area in the brain called the hypothalamus, which in turn controls the pituitary gland, the so-called master gland of the body. Stimulation of the pituitary gland by the hypothalamus leads to the production and release of pituitary hormones that regulate the activity of secondary glands and tissues throughout the body. A specific example is the control of the ovaries and the reproductive cycle. In this case, the pituitary gland releases follicle-stimulating hormone (FSH), resulting in the growth and development of ovarian follicle cells. These cells, under the influence of FSH, begin to synthesize and secrete large amounts of the hormone estrogen. The physiological role of estrogen is to stimulate the growth and development of the mammary glands for eventual lactation, and of the uterine lining, in preparation for fertilization, implantation, and development of the fetus. The ovarian reproductive cycle is characterized by monthly fluctuations in the amount of estrogen released into the blood. After menopause, when the ovaries stop responding to FSH, the level of estrogen in the blood decreases and remains low thereafter. However, because of the endocrine function of adipocytes, obese women have chronically high levels of estrogen in their blood throughout their lives. The constant stimulation of cells in the breast, uterus, and other areas by estrogen and possibly leptin is believed to be the single most important cause of cancer development in these tissues.

Scientists have shown that obese women have much higher levels of estrogen (130 percent more) than do thinner women. A similar relationship is believed to influence the incidence of prostate cancer in men. In this case, the estrogen produced by the adipocytes overstimulates the cells in the prostate gland, thus increasing the risk of cancer development. The discovery of leptin and the endocrine function of fat cells provides a direct link between obesity and the high incidence of cancer in the developed world. Breast and prostate cancers are only two of the many cancers that are likely to be induced by a high-fat diet. Additional cancers, of the pancreas, liver, lung, stomach, and skin, may be attributable to both the elevated levels of sex steroids and to leptin.

High fat content is only one element in the North American diet that predisposes people to cancer. A second, and very important, element is insufficient fiber in the diet. Dietary fiber is thought to protect against cancers in general, but most particularly colorectal cancer. Two epidemiological studies completed in 2003 examined the relationship between dietary fiber and colon cancer. These studies, involving 519,978 Europeans and 33,971 Americans, are unprecedented for their size and scope. Participants in the study completed a dietary questionnaire in 1992–98 and were followed up for cancer incidence. The results showed a clear inverse relationship between the incidence of colon cancer and intake of dietary fiber. In other words, high fiber intake is associated with a low incidence of cancer. No food source of fiber was more protective than others. That is, the fiber could come from bread, vegetables, or breakfast cereal. The authors of the studies concluded that in populations with low-fiber diets, an approximate doubling of total fiber intake from foods could reduce the risk of colorectal cancer by 40 percent. The American and European studies were both published in the May 3, 2003, issue of the medical journal *The Lancet.*

Cancer and Lifestyle

Although cancer risk increases with obesity and with lack of dietary fiber, many people who are not overweight and eat a healthy diet still develop cancer. A striking example is lung cancer induced by the smoke from cigarettes. This type of cancer is the product of a lifestyle that counteracts the beneficial effects of a healthy diet and slim physique. Another lifestyle variable, excessive alcohol consumption, is associated with increased risk of various cancers, particularly liver cancer. Frequent sunbathing without an effective sunscreen is the greatest single cause of skin cancer (melanoma).

The impact of lifestyle is, of course, exacerbated when poor diet, excessive alcohol consumption, and smoking are combined, as is com-

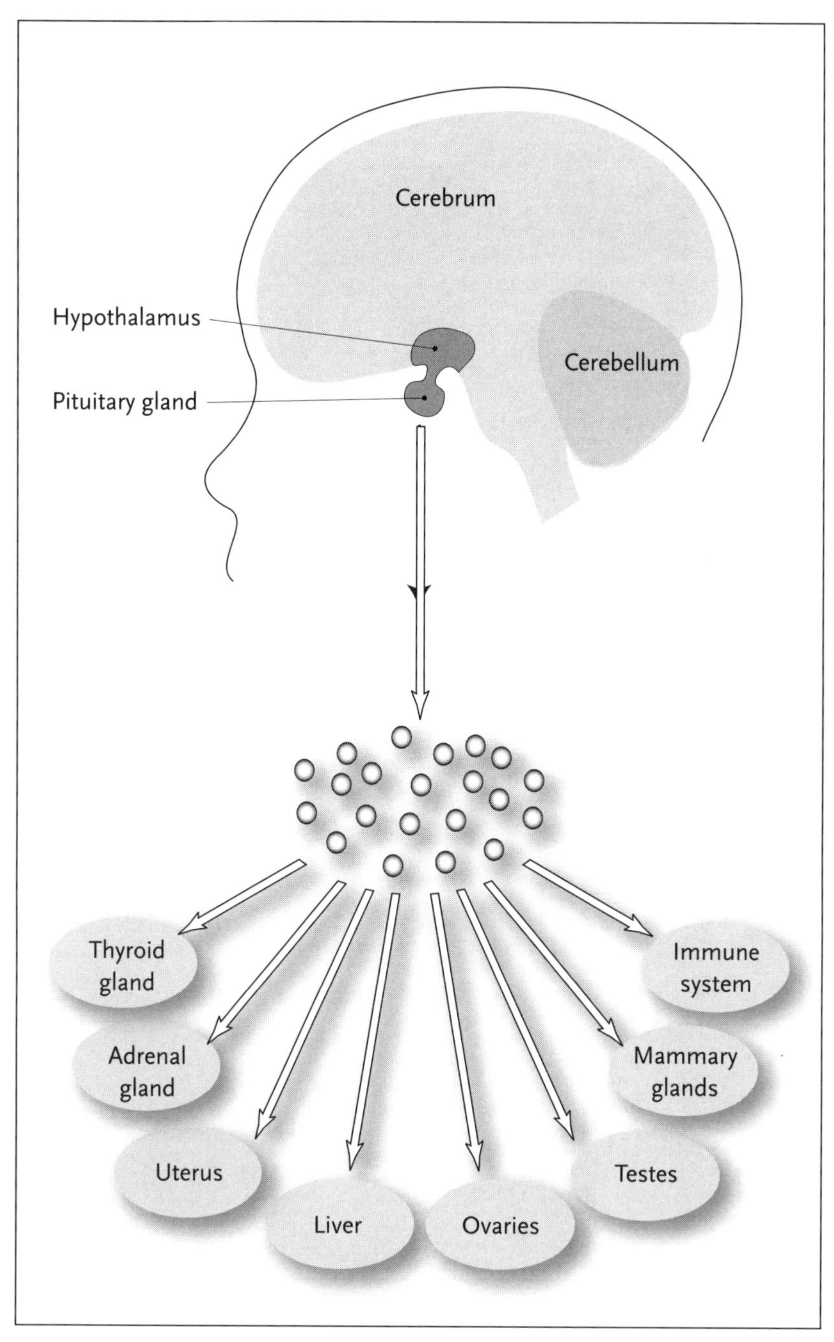

The human endocrine system is controlled by the hypothalamus, which regulates the production and release of various hormones from the pituitary gland. The pituitary hormones, in turn, regulate other glands, tissues, and organs of the body.

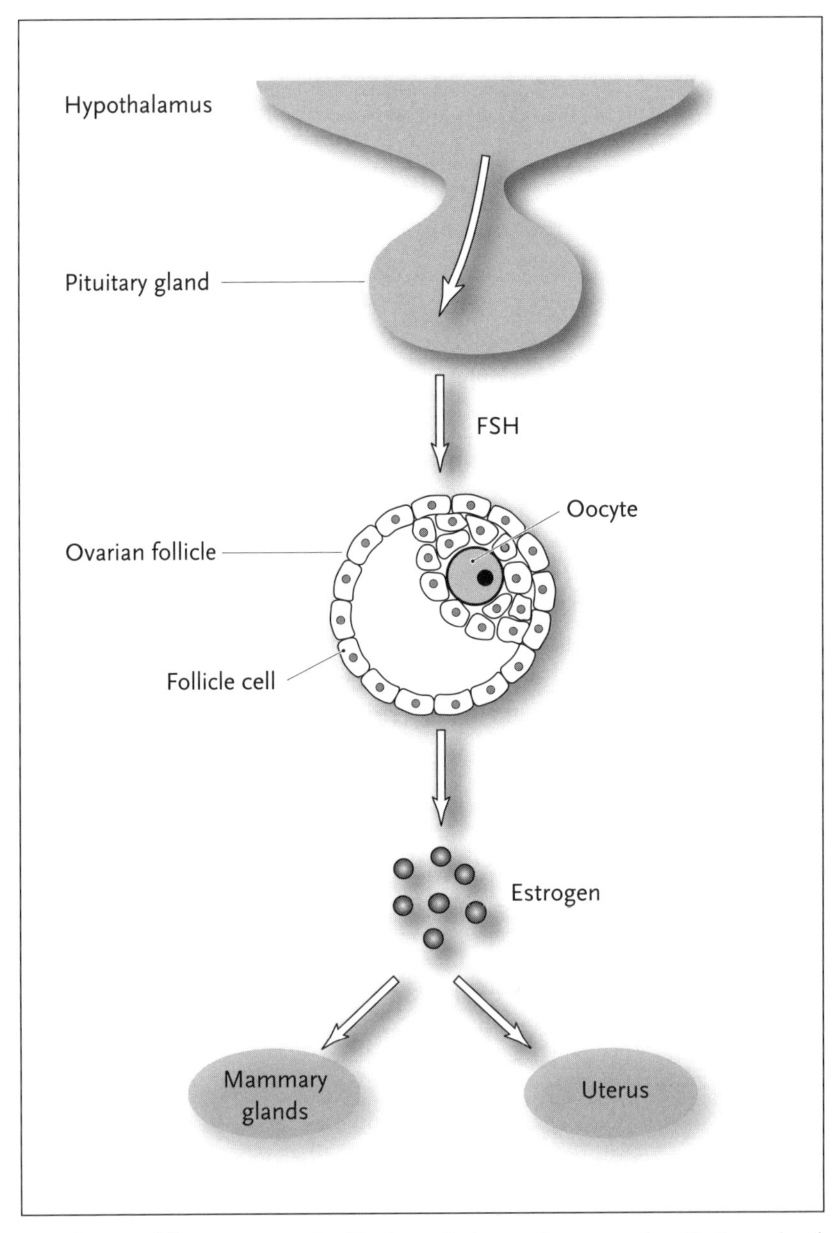

Regulation of the ovarian cycle. The hypothalamus instructs the pituitary gland to release follicle-stimulating hormone (FSH), promoting maturation of ovarian follicle cells, which in turn begin synthesizing and releasing the hormone estrogen. Estrogen induces growth and proliferation of breast and uterine cells.

monly done in North America and Europe. This particular combination almost invariably spells trouble. In rare cases, smokers, for example, have lived long, cancer-free lives, but there are usually compensating elements to their lifestyles. For example, they may not be overweight, or they may have a diet consisting of anticancer foods, such as olive oil, moderate amounts of red wine, and plenty of fruits and vegetables. Such individuals may also have an unusually effective immune system that destroys all cancer cells before they develop into a serious problem.

Cancer and the Environment

There are many agents in the environment that will induce cancers in people who are otherwise healthy and careful about what they eat and drink. Two examples of such carcinogens were described in chapter 4: The first involved a fungal carcinogen that causes liver cancer in people living in the tropics, and the second was asbestos, which damaged the lungs of British factory workers in the 1950s. The incidence of stomach cancer among the Japanese, shown in the table, may be due to the consumption of fish containing high pesticide or mercury residues.

Food additives, pesticides, and herbicides are believed to be responsible for causing cancers. While many of these compounds have been shown to be mutagens in vitro, there is very little evidence thus far to support their role as carcinogens. Much of the difficulty associated with confirming such a link stems from the problem of distinguishing the effects of a specific pesticide or herbicide from other factors, such as obesity or cigarette smoke. While food additives and pesticides may cause cancer, the number of cases resulting from these carcinogens is believed to be very small compared to the quantity arising from dietary practices (such as fat and fiber intake) and lifestyle.

Summary

Cancer is a disease of the genes, but the incidence of this disease is greatly influenced by what we eat and how we live. DNA, though a stable molecule, can be damaged by environmental compounds, radiation, and errors in replication that occur during the cell cycle. The cell has very efficient DNA repair systems, but they can only do so much.

A detailed comparison of cancer rates around the world has shown that most cancers are avoidable. DNA damage, at the heart of cancer induction, can be minimized with a careful attention to diet and lifestyle. A cancer-resistant diet is low in fat and high in fiber, fruits, and vegetables. A cancer-resistant lifestyle includes regular exercise, no smoking, regular use of a sunscreen, and moderate consumption of alcohol. Studies have shown that these simple measures can reduce the incidence of cancer by almost 40 percent, or 4 million cancer cases worldwide each year.

·7·

CLINICAL TRIALS

The fight against cancer is waged on three fronts simultaneously: in research laboratories, where scientists are trying to learn more about cancer cells, in the hospitals where patients are treated with the various therapies described previously, and in clinical trials where new procedures, or modifications to preexisting methods, are tested for their effectiveness. Several hundred such trials are under way worldwide. This chapter will describe a representative sample of trials that were concluded in 2003. We begin with a brief introduction to the organization of clinical trials as they are conducted in North America and Europe.

The Four Phases

Clinical trials are conducted in four phases and are always preceded by research conducted on experimental animals such as mice, rats, or monkeys. The format for preclinical research is informal; it is conducted in a variety of research labs around the world, with the results being published in scientific journals. Formal approval from a governmental regulatory body is not required.

PHASE I CLINICAL TRIAL Pending the outcome of the preclinical research, investigators may apply for permission to try the experiments on human subjects. Applications in the United States are made to the Food and Drug Administration (FDA), the National Institutes of Health (NIH), and the Recombinant DNA Advisory Committee (RAC). RAC was set up by NIH to monitor any research, including clinical trials, dealing with cloning, recombinant DNA, or gene therapy. Phase I trials are conducted on a small number of adult volunteers, usually two to 20, who have given informed consent. That is, the investigators explain the procedure, the possible outcomes, and especially, the dangers associated with the procedure before the subjects sign a consent form. The purpose of the Phase I trial is to determine the overall effect the treatment has on humans. A treatment that works well in monkeys or mice may not work at all on humans. Similarly, a treatment that appears safe in lab animals may be toxic, even deadly, when given to humans. Since most clinical trials are testing a new drug of some kind, the first priority is to determine a safe dosage for humans. Consequently, subjects in the Phase I trial are given a range of doses, all of which, even the high dose, are less than the highest dose given to experimental animals. If the results from the Phase I trial are promising, the investigators may apply for permission to proceed to Phase II.

PHASE II CLINICAL TRIAL Having established the general protocol, or procedure, the investigators now try to replicate the encouraging results from Phase I, but with a much larger number of subjects (100–300). Only with a large number of subjects is it possible to prove the treatment has an effect. In addition, dangerous side effects may have been missed in Phase I because of a small sample size. The results from Phase II will determine how safe the procedure is and whether it works or not. If the statistics show that treatment is effective and toxicity is low, the investigators may apply for permission to proceed to Phase III.

PHASE III CLINICAL TRIAL Based on Phase II results the procedure may look very promising, but before it can be used as a routine treatment it must be tested on thousands of patients at a variety of research centers. This is the expensive part of bringing a new drug or therapy to market, costing millions, sometimes billions, of dollars. It is for this reason that Phase III clinical trials invariably have the financial backing of large pharmaceutical or biotechnology companies. If the results of the Phase II trial are confirmed in Phase III, the FDA will approve the use of the drug for routine treatment. The use of the drug or treatment now passes into an informal Phase IV trial.

PHASE IV CLINICAL TRIAL Even though the treatment has gained formal approval, its performance is monitored for very-long-term effects, sometimes stretching on for 10 to 20 years. In this way, the FDA retains the power to recall the drug long after it has become a part of standard medical procedure. It can happen that in the long term, the drug costs more than an alternative, in which case, health insurance providers may refuse to cover the cost of the treatment.

Breast Cancer

TUMOR DETECTION Three recent trials assessed the value of magnetic resonance imaging (MRI) in screening women for breast cancer. These studies examined whether MRI might be a more effective screening tool than mammography. The results were presented at the annual meeting of the American Society of Clinical Oncology (ASCO), held in Chicago on June 2, 2003. Effectiveness was measured in two ways: Sensitivity (how well the procedure detects a cancer when one is present), and specificity (how well the procedure avoids false positives, or a result suggesting a tumor is present when there is none). If screening suggested the presence of cancer, a biopsy was performed to confirm or deny the finding.

In the first study, which ran from November 1999 to August 2002, researchers in the Netherlands (the Dutch MRI Screening Study) evaluated 1,911 high-risk women at several centers throughout the country. The women received a clinical breast exam (CBE) twice yearly, a yearly mammography, and a yearly MRI. Researchers evaluated each woman's mammography results independently of her MRI results, so if one imaging system suggested the presence of cancer the evaluator would not be biased towards expecting to see signs of cancer from the other system. Each woman in the study was followed for about two years. During this time, investigators found invasive breast cancers or noninvasive tumors (ductal carcinoma in situ) in 40 of the women. Forty-six percent of the tumors were small (1 centimeter or less) and 77 percent were confined to the breast. While the clinical breast exam detected 16 percent of the tumors and mammography found 36 percent, MRI sensitivity was found to be 71 percent. MRI sensitivity was even more pronounced in cases of invasive cancer (spread beyond the layer of tissue in which it developed), with 20 percent found by CBE, 26 percent by mammography, and 83 percent by MRI. Although more sensitive, MRI was less specific than the other two methods, leading to a greater number of false positives. Twelve percent of the time, MRI suggested that there was a cancer when there was none, compared to 5 percent for mammography and 3 percent for CBE.

In a second trial, conducted at the University of Bonn in 1998 and involving 462 women, researchers have found that MRI offers a sensitivity of 96 percent, compared to 25 percent for CBE and 43 percent for mammography. Moreover, in contrast to the Dutch study, this trial found that MRI actually resulted in fewer cases of false positives than the other forms of screening, leading the German researchers to suggest that MRI should replace mammography as a screening tool for high-risk women.

In a third study, which did not directly compare MRI with other forms of breast cancer screening, researchers at the Memorial Sloan-Kettering Cancer Center in New York reviewed medical and radiology reports for 54 women with BRCA mutations who had 115 MRI exams between 1998 and 2002. They found that MRI was 100 percent sensitive for correctly detecting breast cancer (finding a tumor when there was one), but only 83 percent specific. That is, 17 percent of MRI's results were false positives. The investigators concluded that MRI sensitivity is encouraging, but that the high false-positive rate limits its use as a routine practice.

Investigators from all of the trials agree that while MRI looks very promising, further research will be needed to reduce the number of false positives before it can be recommended as a routine procedure.

TAMOXIFEN TREATMENT FOR BREAST CANCER A study published in the February 19, 2003, issue of the *Journal of the National Cancer Institute* concluded that women at high risk for breast cancer who took the drug tamoxifen (a compound that blocks the cell-stimulatory effects of estrogen) were less likely to be diagnosed with benign (noncancerous) breast conditions than women who took a placebo. The study participants, enrolled in the Breast Cancer Prevention Trial at the Cancer Research Network in Plantation, Florida, took tamoxifen for five years.

The researchers found that the risk of developing benign tumors was reduced by 28 percent for women in the tamoxifen group. In addition, women treated with tamoxifen had 29 percent fewer biopsies than women who received a placebo. The reduction in biopsies was seen predominantly in premenopausal women. The results suggest that tamoxifen inhibits the formation of early breast abnormalities, such as hyperplasia, that could develop into metastatic or invasive cancer.

Chemotherapy

Dr. Sandra Swain, chief of the National Cancer Institute's Cancer Therapeutics Branch, recently concluded a study evaluating the side effects of doxorubicin (Adriamycin), widely used in cancer chemotherapy. Doxorubicin is a highly effective anticancer drug but it is suspected of increasing patients' risk of congestive heart failure (CHF). In CHF the heart has trouble beating normally because of damage to the heart muscle. To evaluate the risk of CHF from treatment with doxorubicin, Swain and her colleagues looked back at the medical records of 630 patients who received a placebo instead of dexrazoxane (a drug that blocks doxorubicin side effects) in three trials conducted in the 1990s. Patients were followed up to find out whether they had experienced CHF at any time, either while they were enrolled in the study or later.

A total of 32 of the 630 patients (5 percent) had doxorubicin-related CHF. In 11 cases the CHF occurred while the patient was enrolled in the trial; in the other cases, it occurred later. Ten of 172 patients (6 percent) aged over 65 experienced the problem, compared with 22 of 458 patients (5 percent) aged under 65. It was estimated that the percentage of patients with doxorubicin-related CHF rose with increasing doses of the drug. At a dose of 550 mg/m^2, they estimated that 26 percent of patients would experience this adverse event. The estimate rose to 48 percent at a dose of 700 mg/m^2. A total of 149 patients (24 percent) experienced a "cardiac event" (either CHF or a test result indicating that the heart is pumping less blood than normal) while enrolled in the study. Swain and her colleagues estimated that, at a dose of 550 mg/m^2, 65 percent of patients would have a cardiac event. Dr. Swain recommends that all patients with metastatic breast cancer who receive more than 300 mg/m^2 of doxorubicin also receive dexrazoxane to minimize the risk of heart problems. However, the use of dexrazoxane is only approved for breast cancer patients with disease that has spread, and only after they have received a cumulative dose of doxorubicin of 300 mg/m^2.

Colon Cancer

A study conducted at the University of North Carolina, Chapel Hill, and at the Norris Cotton Cancer Center in Lebanon, New Hampshire, has shown that taking aspirin every day for as little as three years reduces the occurrence of colorectal polyps by 19 percent to 35 percent. The results were published on March 5, 2003, in the *New England Journal of Medicine.* These data confirm numerous earlier observational studies suggesting that people who regularly take aspirin have lower rates of colorectal adenomas. Adenomas are abnormal growths (polyps) that precede the development of most colorectal cancers.

Previous studies have shown that people who regularly take aspirin to treat conditions such as arthritis have lower rates of colorectal polyps, colorectal cancer, and colorectal cancer deaths. Based on these results, as well as on animal models and laboratory data, the National Cancer Institute (NCI) supported the current trial, in which people were randomly assigned to aspirin or a placebo and followed for a several years. The study suggests that daily aspirin may be an appropriate supplement to regular surveillance procedures in individuals who are at risk of developing colon cancer. The trial participants were adults with either a previous colorectal adenoma or previous early-stage cancer successfully treated with surgery.

Lung Cancer

Non-small-cell lung cancer (NSCLC) accounts for about 80 percent of all lung cancer cases. The average five-year survival rate is about 50 percent for patients whose NSCLC is found early and treated with surgery before it has spread to other organs. In advanced-stage disease, chemotherapy offers modest improvements in median survival, although overall survival is poor.

Docetaxel, a drug that inhibits mitosis, is the current standard treatment for NSCLC that recurs after chemotherapy. In previous studies, docetaxel improved survival compared with other chemotherapy drugs or observation, but was found to cause severe side effects, such as fever and infections. Other studies have suggested that the experimental drug pemetrexed might be an effective alternative to docetaxel. Pemetrexed is an enzyme inhibitor that interferes with the body's production of vitamin B (folic acid), which is essential for normal cell growth.

In the current study, which ran from March 2001 to February 2002 at Indiana University in Indianapolis, 571 patients with recurrent NSCLC were given docetaxel or pemetrexed in a phase III clinical trial (see chapter 8). As of May 2003 the survival rate of the patients was about the same whether they were treated with pemetrexed (8.3 months) or docetaxel (7.9 months). Patients in both treatment groups had about a 30 percent chance of surviving for one year. Survival was no different between the two groups of patients, but those treated with pemetrexed were less likely to suffer from fever and infections caused by low levels of white blood cells. They were also less likely to be hospitalized for fever or other side effects or to need treatment to stimulate production of white blood cells. In addition, patients treated with pemetrexed suffered less hair loss and less numbness in the arms and legs.

Melanoma

Scientists at the National Cancer Institute (NCI) have found a new method for modifying the immune system of cancer patients to induce cancer regression. By inhibiting a molecule associated with T lymphocytes called cytotoxic T lymphocyte-associated antigen 4 (CTLA-4), the immune system is able to attack some patients' tumors. CTLA-4 was inhibited with an antibody leading to tumor shrinkage in patients with metastatic melanoma. In addition to the tumor shrinkage, the treatment also induced evidence of autoimmunity, that is, signs that the immune system was attacking not only tumors, but normal tissue as well. However, treatment with steroids completely eliminated all symptoms of autoimmunity that occurred in the trial.

The 14 patients in the study received an antibody that blocks CTLA-4 activity, plus a cancer vaccine made up of a small segment of a protein found on the surface of melanoma cells. The hope is that the vaccine will stimulate the immune system to attack cancer cells, but in previous clinical trials, this type of vaccine alone did not cause melanoma tumors to shrink. Researchers speculated that CTLA-4's inhibition of T cell activity might be in part responsible for this lack of an effective immune response. Blocking CTLA-4 did indeed improve the response to treatment. In two of the patients in the study, all tumors, which included significant metastases in the lung and brain, disappeared completely. A partial response, defined as a 30 percent to 100 percent decrease in tumor size, was seen in one additional patient. In another two patients, some tumors decreased in size, but other tumors continued to grow. Six patients, including all of those whose tumors regressed, experienced significant autoimmune effects in normal tissues in response to the treatment. The enhanced activity of immune cells in these patients led to symptoms including skin rashes, inflammation of the colon, and hepatitis. With treatment, all of these symptoms were resolved.

Metastasis

When a tumor spreads to the vertebrae, the spinal cord can be compressed and can cause some patients to lose mobility or bladder control. Researchers wondered whether surgery to remove the tumor in addition to radiation would benefit cancer patients by alleviating the pressure and stabilizing the spine. Spinal cord compression occurs in 10 to 20 percent of all cancer patients, especially lung, prostate, and breast cancer patients.

A randomized phase III study of 101 patients compared the advantages of surgery combined with radiation as opposed to radiation alone in relieving spinal cord compression. In this NCI-funded study, as much tumor as possible was removed from the spinal columns of 50 patients, who were then treated with radiation. Fifty-one patients received radiation only. Patients who received surgery in addition to radiation for their spinal compression showed a marked improvement in their ability to walk as compared to patients receiving radiation only.

Surgically treated patients also maintained continence for a much longer period. Sixteen patients in each group entered the study unable to walk. Nine patients treated with surgery and radiation regained the ability to walk (56 percent), compared to only three receiving radiation alone (19 percent). The study was stopped early due to the overwhelming benefits of surgery combined with radiation.

.8. RESOURCE CENTER

Eukaryote Cell Primer

Life on Earth began 3.5 billion years ago in the form of single cells that appeared in the oceans. These cells evolved into ancestral prokaryotes and, about 2 billion years ago, gave rise to Archaea, bacteria, and eukaryotes, the three major divisions of life in the world. Eukaryotes, in turn, gave rise to plants, animals, protozoans, and fungi. Each of these groups represents a distinct phylogenetic kingdom. The archaea and bacteria represent a fifth kingdom, known as the monera or prokaryotes. Archaea and bacteria are very similar anatomically; both lack a true nucleus and internal organelles. A prokaryote genome is a single, circular piece of naked DNA called a chromosome, containing fewer than 5,000 genes. Eukaryotes (meaning "true nuclei") are much more complex, having many membrane-bounded organelles. These include a nucleus, nucleolus, endoplasmic reticulum (ER), Golgi complex, mitochondria, lysosomes, and peroxisomes.

The eukaryote nucleus, bounded by a double phospholipid membrane, contains a DNA (deoxyribonucleic acid) genome on two or more linear chromosomes, each of which may contain up to 10,000 genes. The nucleus also contains an assembly plant for ribosomal subunits called the nucleolus. The endoplasmic reticulum (ER) and the Golgi complex work together to glycosylate proteins and lipids (attach sugar molecules to the proteins and lipids producing glycoproteins and glycolipids), most of which are destined for the cell membrane to form a molecular "forest" known as the glycocalyx. The glycoproteins and

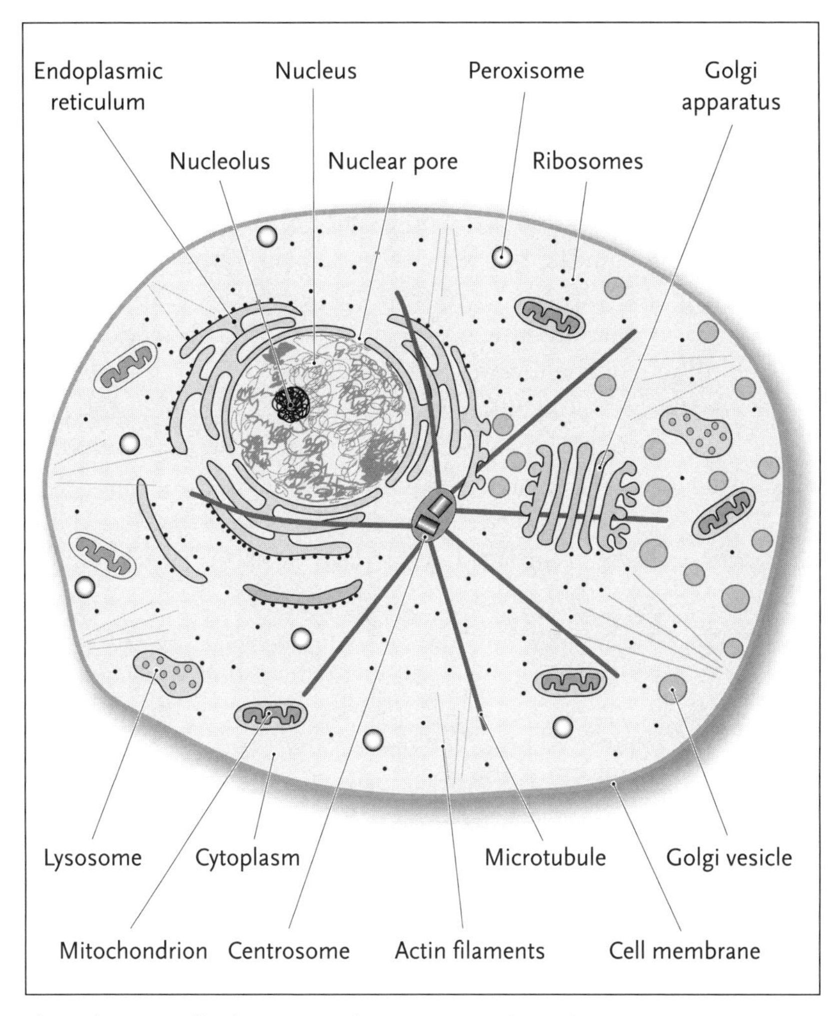

The eukaryote cell. The structural components shown here are present in organisms as diverse as protozoans, plants, and animals. The nucleus contains the DNA genome and an assembly plant for ribosomal subunits (the nucleolus). The endoplasmic reticulum (ER) and the Golgi work together to modify proteins, most of which are destined for the cell membrane. These proteins are sent to the membrane in Golgi vesicles. Mitochondria provide the cell with energy in the form of ATP. Ribosomes, some of which are attached to the ER, synthesize proteins. Lysosomes and peroxisomes recycle cellular material and molecules. The microtubules and centrosome form the spindle apparatus for moving chromosomes to the daughter cells during cell division. Actin filaments and a weblike structure consisting of intermediate filaments (not shown) form the cytoskeleton.

glycolipids travel from the ER to the Golgi, and from the Golgi to the cell surface, in membrane-bounded vesicles that form by budding off the organelle by exocytosis. Thus, the cytoplasm contains many transport vesicles that originate from the ER and Golgi. The Golgi vesicles bud off the outer chamber, or the one farthest from the ER. Mitochondria, once free-living prokaryotes, and the only other organelle with a double membrane, provide the cell with energy in the form of adenosine triphosphate (ATP). The production of ATP is carried out by an assembly of metal-containing proteins called the electron transport chain, located in the mitochondrion inner membrane. Ribosomes, some of which are attached to the ER, synthesize proteins. Lysosomes and peroxisomes recycle cellular material and molecules. The microtubules and centrosome form the spindle apparatus for moving chromosomes to the daughter cells during cell division. Actin filaments and a weblike structure consisting of intermediate filaments form the cytoskeleton.

MOLECULES OF THE CELL

Cells are biochemical entities that synthesize many thousands of molecules. Studying these chemicals and the biochemistry of the cell would be a daunting task were it not for the fact that most of the chemical variation is based on six types of molecules, which are assembled into just four types of macromolecules. The six basic molecules are amino acids, phosphate, glycerol, sugars, fatty acids, and nucleotides. Amino acids have a simple core structure consisting of an amino group, a carboxyl group, and a variable R group attached to a carbon atom. There are 20 different kinds of amino acids, each with a unique R group. Phosphates are extremely important molecules that are used in the construction or modification of many other molecules. They are also used to store chemical-bond energy. Glycerol is a simple three-carbon alcohol that is an important component of cell membranes and fat reservoirs. Sugars are extremely versatile molecules that are used as an energy source and for structural purposes. Glucose, a six-carbon sugar, is the primary energy source for most cells and it is the principal sugar used to glycosylate proteins and lipids for the production of the glycocalyx. Plants have exploited the structural potential of sugars in their production of cellulose and, thus, wood, bark, grasses, and reeds are polymers of glucose and other monosaccharides. Ribose, a five-carbon sugar, is a

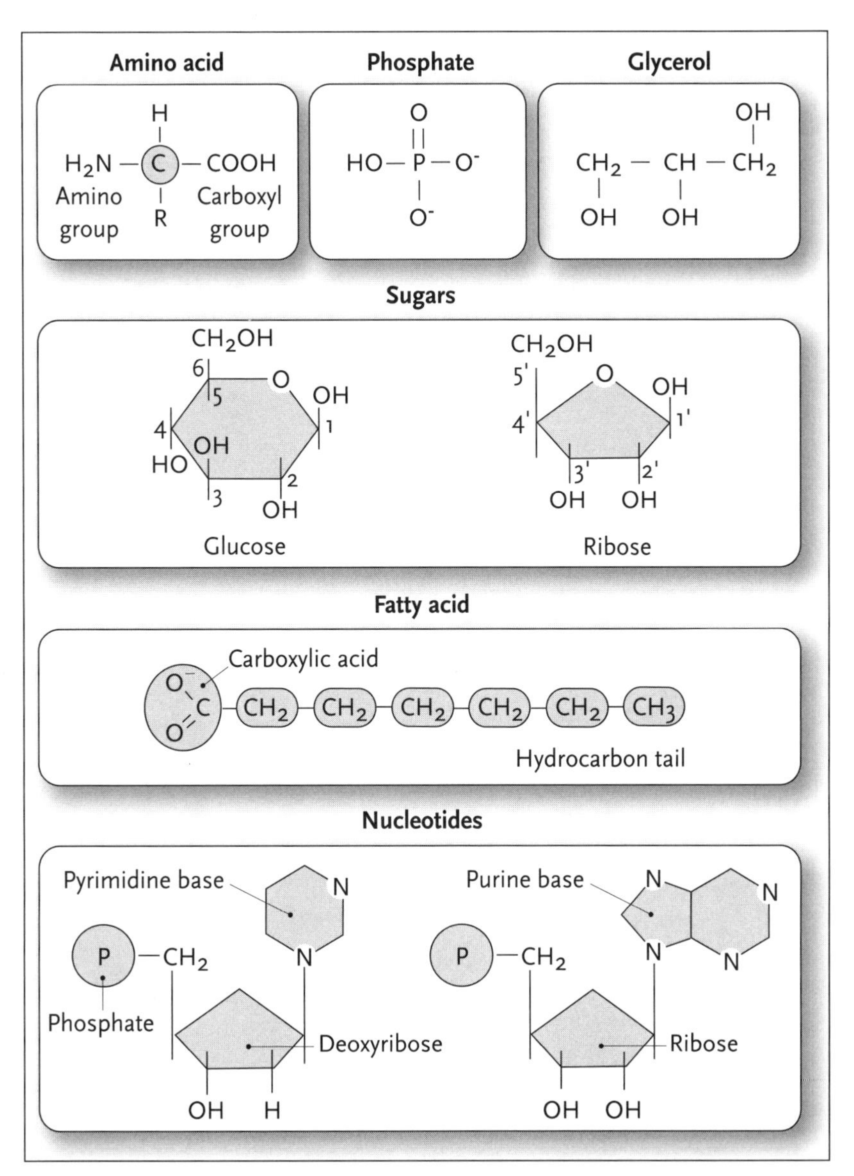

Molecules of the cell. Amino acids are the building blocks for proteins. Phosphate is an important component of many other molecules, and is added to proteins to modify their behavior. Glycerol is a three-carbon alcohol that is an important ingredient in cell membranes and fat. Sugars like glucose are a primary energy source for most cells and also have many structural functions. Fatty acids are involved in the production of cell membranes and storage of fat. Nucleotides are the building blocks of DNA and RNA.

component of nucleic acids, as well as ATP. Ribose carbons are numbered as 1' (1 prime), 2' and so on. Consequently, references to nucleic acids, which include ribose, often refer to the 3' or 5' carbon. Fatty acids consist of a carboxyl group (when ionized it becomes a carboxylic acid) linked to a hydrophobic hydrocarbon tail. These molecules are used in the construction of cell membranes and fat.

Nucleotides are building blocks for DNA and RNA (ribonucleic acid). Nucleotides consist of three components: a phosphate, a ribose sugar, and a nitrogenous (nitrogen containing) ring compound that behaves as a base in solution. Nucleotide bases appear in two forms: A single-ring nitrogenous base called a pyrimidine, and a double-ringed base called a purine. There are two kinds of purines (adenine and guanine), and three pyrimidines (uracil, cytosine, and thymine). Uracil is specific to RNA, substituting for thymine. In addition, RNA nucleotides contain ribose, whereas DNA nucleotides contain deoxyribose (hence their names). Ribose has a hydroxyl (OH) group attached to both the 2' and 3' carbons, whereas deoxyribose is missing the 2' hydroxyl group. ATP, the molecule that is used by all cells as a source of energy, is a ribose nucleotide consisting of the purine base adenine and three phosphates attached to the 5' carbon of the ribose sugar. The phosphates are labeled α (alpha), β (beta) and γ (gamma), and are linked to the carbon in a tandem order, beginning with α. The energy stored by this molecule is carried by the covalent bonds of the β and γ phosphates. Breaking these bonds sequentially releases the energy they contain, while converting ATP to adenosine diphosphate (ADP) and then to adenosine monophosphate (AMP). AMP is converted back to ATP by mitochondria.

MACROMOLECULES OF THE CELL

The six basic molecules are used by all cells to construct five essential macromolecules. These include proteins, RNA, DNA, phospholipids, and sugar polymers, known as polysaccharides. Amino acids are linked together by peptide bonds to construct a protein. A peptide bond is formed by linking the carboxyl end of one amino acid to the amino end of second amino acid. Thus, once constructed, every protein has an amino end and a carboxyl end. An average protein may consist of 300–400 amino acids. Nucleic acids are macromolecules constructed

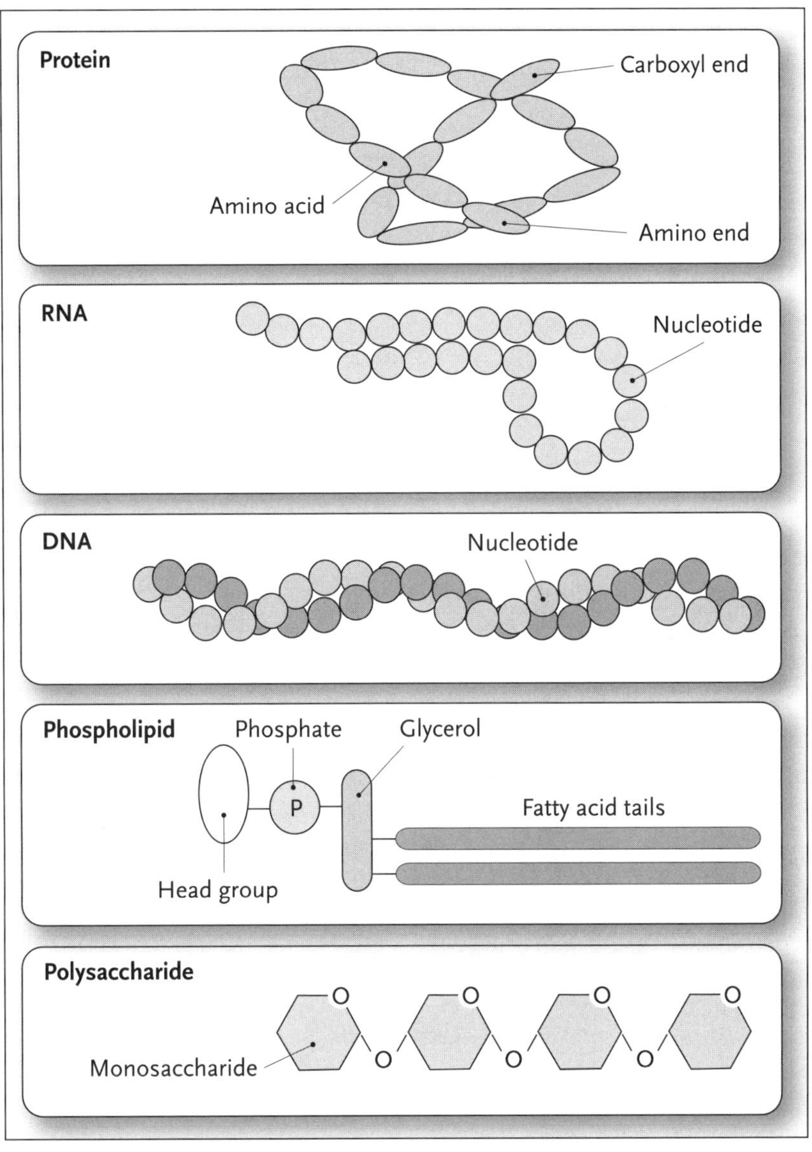

Macromolecules of the cell. Protein is made from amino acids linked together to form a long chain that can fold up into a three-dimensional structure. RNA and DNA are long chains of nucleotides. RNA is generally single-stranded, but can form localized double-stranded regions. DNA is a double-stranded helix, with one strand coiling around the other. A phospholipid is composed of a hydrophilic head-group, a phosphate, a glycerol molecule, and two hydrophobic fatty-acid tails. Polysaccharides are sugar polymers.

from nucleotides. The 5' phosphate of one nucleotide is linked to the 3' OH of a second nucleotide. Additional nucleotides are always linked to the 3' OH of the last nucleotide in the chain. Consequently, the growth of the chain is said to be in the 5' to 3' direction. RNA nucleotides are adenine, uracil, cytosine, and guanine. A typical RNA molecule consists of 2,000 to 3,000 nucleotides; it is generally single stranded, but can form localized double-stranded regions. RNA is involved in the synthesis of proteins and is a structural and enzymatic component of ribosomes. DNA, a double-stranded nucleic acid, encodes cellular genes and is constructed from adenine, thymine, cytosine, and guanine deoxyribonucleotides (dATP, dTTP, dCTP and dGTP, where "d" indicates deoxyribose). The two DNA strands coil around each other like strands in a piece of rope, and for this reason the molecule is known as the double helix. DNA is an extremely large macromolecule, typically consisting of more than 1 million nucleotide pairs (or base pairs). Double-stranded DNA forms when two chains of nucleotides interact through the formation of chemical bonds between complementary base pairs. The chemistry of the bases is such that adenine pairs with thymine and cytosine pairs with guanine. For stability, the two strands are antiparallel, that is, the orientation of one strand is in the 5' to 3' direction, while the complementary strand runs 3' to 5'. Phospholipids, the main component of cell membranes, are composed of a polar head group (usually an alcohol), a phosphate, glycerol, and two hydrophobic fatty-acid tails. Fat that is stored in the body as an energy reserve has a

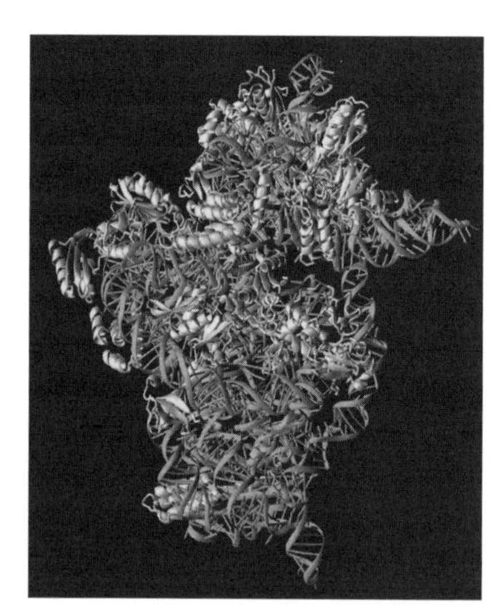

Molecule model of the 30S ribosomal subunit, which consists of protein (light gray corkscrew structures) and RNA (coiled ladders). The overall shape of the molecule is determined by the RNA, which is also responsible for the catalytic function of the ribosome. *(Courtesy of V. Ramakrishnan, MRC Laboratory of Molecular Biology, Cambridge)*

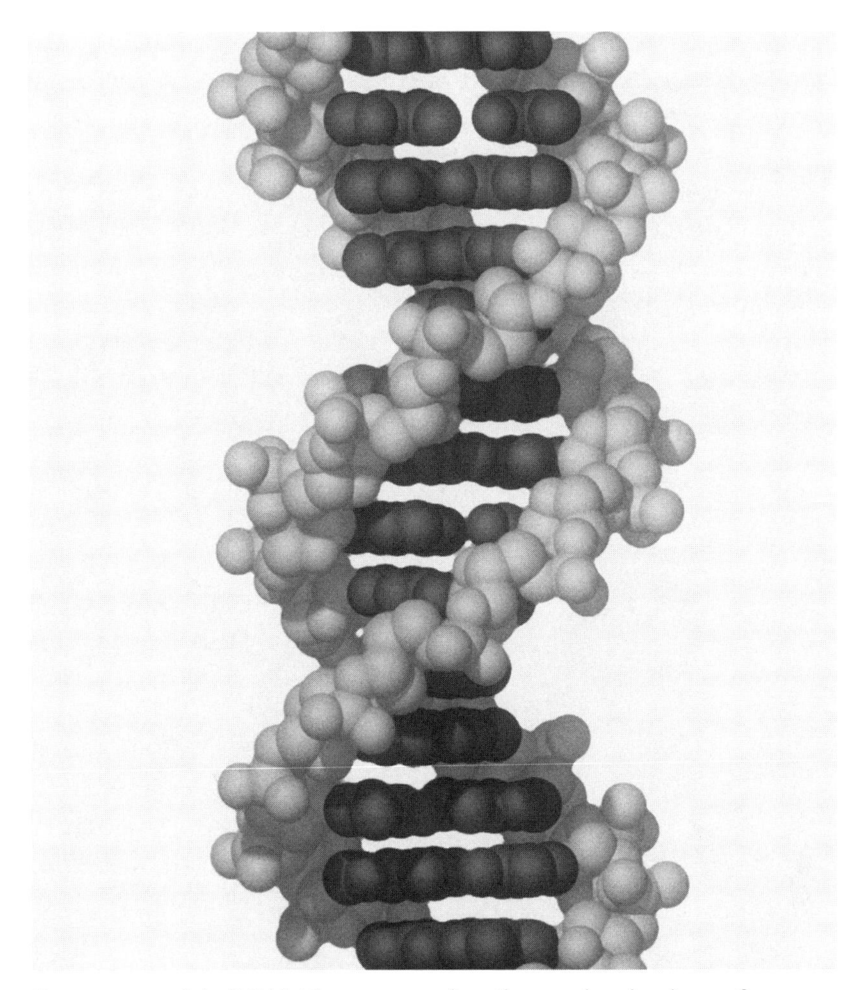

Computer model of DNA. The two strands coil around each other to form a helix that, when looking on it from above, coils to the right. The spherical structures in this image represent the various atoms in the sugars and bases (dark gray), and phosphates (light gray). *(Kenneth Eward/BioGrafx/Photo Researchers, Inc.)*

structure similar to a phospholipid, being composed of three fatty acid chains attached to a molecule of glycerol. The third fatty acid takes the place of the phosphate and head group of a phospholipid. Sugars are polymerized to form chains of two or more monosaccharides. Disaccharides (two monosaccharides) and oligosaccharides (three to 12 monosaccharides) are attached to proteins and lipids destined for the glycocalyx. Polysaccharides, such as glycogen and starch, may contain several hundred monosaccharides and are stored in cells as an energy reserve.

THE CELL CYCLE

Cells inherited the power of reproduction from prebiotic bubbles that split in half at regular intervals under the influence of the turbulent environment that characterized the Earth more than 3 billion years ago. This pattern of turbulent fragmentation followed by a brief period of calm is now a regular behavior pattern of every cell. Even today, after 3 billion years, many cells still divide every 20 minutes.

The regular alternation between division and calm has come to be known as the cell cycle. In studying this cycle, scientists have recognized different states of calm and different ways in which a cell can divide. The calm state of the cell cycle, referred to as interphase, is divided into three sub-phases called Gap 1 (G_1), S phase (a period of DNA synthesis) and Gap 2 (G_2). The conclusion of interphase, and with it the termination of G_2, occurs with division of the cell and a return to G_1. Cells may leave the cycle by entering a special phase called G_0. Some cells, such as postmitotic neurons in an animal's brain, remain in G_0 for the life of the organism.

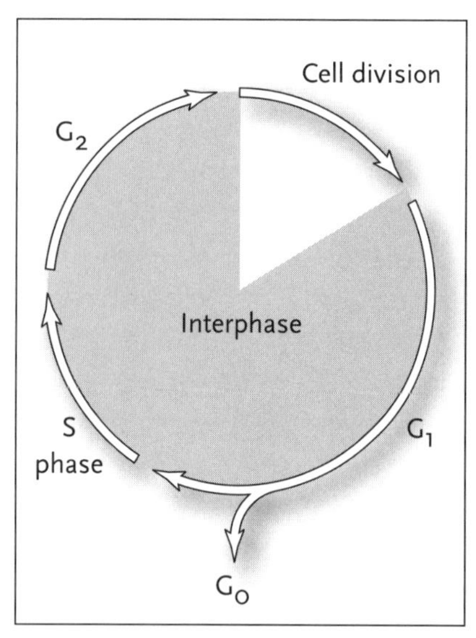

The cell cycle. Most cells spend their time cycling between a state of calm (interphase) and cell division. Interphase is further divided into three subphases: Gap 1 (G_1), S phase (DNA synthesis), and Gap 2 (G_2). Cells may exit the cycle by entering a special phase called G_0.

Although interphase is a period of relative calm, the cell grows continuously during this period, working hard to prepare for the next round of division. Two notable events are the duplication of the spindle (the centrosome and associated microtubules), a structure that is crucial for the movement of the chromosomes during cell division, and the appearance of an enzyme called maturation promoting factor (MPF) at the end of G_2. MPF phosphorylates histones. Histones are proteins that bind to the DNA, which when phosphorylated, compacts (or condenses) the chromosomes in preparation for cell division. MPF is also responsible for the breakdown of the nuclear membrane. When cell division is complete, MPF disappears, allowing the chromosomes to decondense and the nuclear envelope to re-form. Completion of a normal cell cycle always involves the division of a cell into two daughter cells. This can occur by a process known as mitosis, which is intended for cell multiplication, and by a second process known as meiosis, which is intended for sexual reproduction.

MITOSIS

Mitosis is used by all free-living eukaryotes (protozoans) as a means of asexual reproduction. The growth of a plant or an animal is also accomplished with this form of cell division. Mitosis is divided into four stages: prophase, metaphase, anaphase, and telophase. All of these stages are marked out in accordance with the behavior of the nucleus and the chromosomes. Prophase marks the period during which the duplicated chromosomes begin condensation and the two centrosomes begin moving to opposite poles of the cell. Under the microscope, the chromosomes become visible as X-shaped structures, which are the two duplicated chromosomes, often called sister chromatids. A special region of each chromosome, called a centromere, holds the chromatids together. Proteins bind to the centromere to form a structure called the kinetochore. Metaphase is a period during which the chromosomes are sorted out and aligned between the two centrosomes. By this time, the nuclear membrane has completely broken down. The two centrosomes and the microtubules fanning out between them form the mitotic spindle. The area in between the spindles, where the chromosomes are aligned, is often referred to as the metaphase plate. Some of the microtubules make contact with the kinetochores, while others overlap, with motor proteins situated in between. Eukaryotes are normally diploid, so a cell would have two copies of each chromosome, one from the mother and one from the father. Anaphase is characterized by the movement of

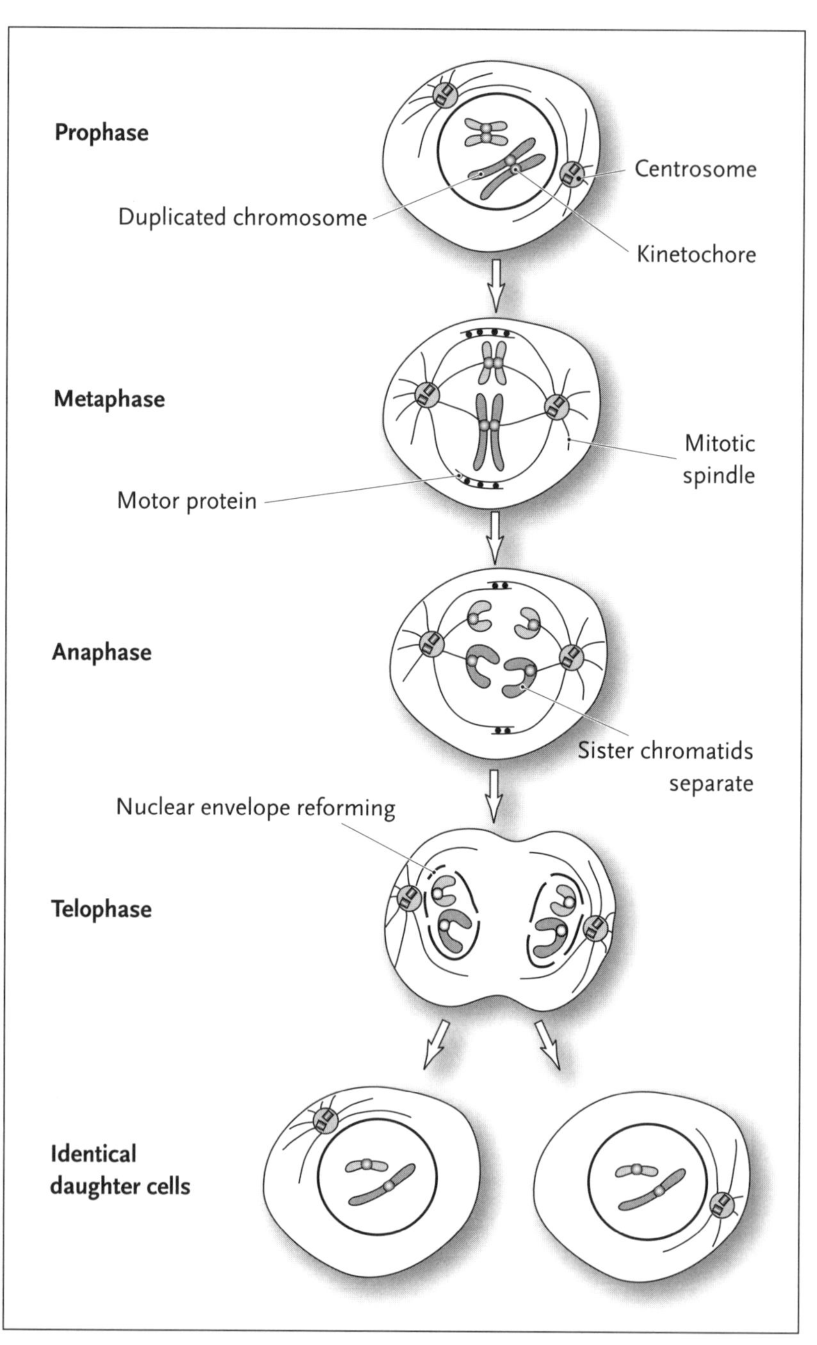

Mitosis. Principal stages deal with the movement and partitioning of the chromosomes between the future daughter cells. For clarity, only two chromosomes are shown.

the duplicated chromosomes to opposite poles of the cell. The first step is the release of an enzyme that breaks the bonds holding the kinetochores together, thus allowing the sister chromatids to separate from each other while remaining bound to their respective microtubules. Motor proteins then move along the microtuble, dragging the chromosomes to opposite ends of the cell. Using energy supplied by ATP, the motor proteins break the microtubule down as it drags the chromosome along, so that the microtubule is gone by the time the chromosome reaches the spindle pole. Throughout this process, the motor proteins and the chromosome manage to stay one step ahead of the disintegrating microtubule. The overlapping microtubules aid movement of the chromosomes toward the poles as another type of motor protein pushes the microtubules in opposite directions, effectively forcing the centrosomes toward the poles. This accounts for the greater overlap of microtubules in metaphase as compared with anaphase. During telophase, the daughter chromosomes arrive at the spindle poles and decondense to form the relaxed chromatin characteristic of interphase nuclei. The nuclear envelope begins forming around the chromosomes, marking the end of mitosis. During the same period, a contractile ring, made of the proteins myosin and actin, begins pinching the parental cell in two. This stage, separate from mitosis, is called cytokinesis, and leads to the formation of two daughter cells, each with one nucleus.

MEIOSIS

Unlike mitosis, which leads to the growth of an organism, meiosis is intended for sexual reproduction and occurs exclusively in ovaries and testes. Eukaryotes, being diploid, receive chromosomes from both parents; if gametes were produced using mitosis, a catastrophic growth in the number of chromosomes would occur each time a sperm fertilized an egg. Meiosis is a special form of cell division that produces haploid gametes (eggs and sperm), each possessing half as many chromosomes as the diploid cell. When haploid gametes fuse, they produce an embryo with the correct number of chromosomes.

The existence of meiosis was first suggested 100 years ago when microbiologists counted the number chromosomes in somatic and germ cells. The roundworm, for example, was found to have four chromosomes in its somatic cells but only two in its gametes. Many other studies also compared the amount of DNA in nuclei from somatic cells and gonads, always with same result: The amount of DNA in somatic cells is exactly double the amount in fully mature gametes. To understand how this could be, scientists studied cell division in the gonads and were able to show that meiosis occurs as two rounds of cell division with only one round of DNA synthesis. The two rounds of division were called meiosis I and meiosis II, and scientists observed that both could be divided into the same four stages known to occur in mitosis. Indeed, meiosis II is virtually identical to a mitotic division. Meiosis I resembles mitosis, but close examination shows three important differences: gene swapping occurs between homologous chromosomes in prophase; homologs (that is, two homologous chromosomes) remain paired at metaphase, instead of lining up at the plate as is done in mitosis; and the kinetochores do not separate at anaphase.

Homologous chromosomes are two identical chromosomes that come from different parents. For example, humans have 23 chromosomes from the father and the same 23 from the mother. We each have a maternal chromosome 1 and a paternal chromosome 1; they carry the same genes but specify slightly different traits. Chromosome 1 may carry the gene for eye color, but the maternal version, or allele, may specify blue eyes, whereas the paternal allele specifies brown. During prophase, homologous pairs exchange large numbers of genes by swapping whole pieces of chromosome. Thus one of the maternal chromatids (gray in the figure) ends up with a piece of paternal chromosome, and a paternal chromatid receives the corresponding piece of maternal chromosome. Mixing genetic material in this way is unique to meiosis, and it is one of the reasons sexual reproduction has been such a powerful evolutionary force.

During anaphase of meiosis I, the kinetochores do not separate as they do in mitosis. The effect of this is to separate the maternal and paternal chromosomes by sending them to different daughter cells, although the segregation is random. That is, the daughter cells receive a random assortment of maternal and paternal chromosomes, rather than one daughter cell receiving all paternal chromosomes and the other all maternal chromosomes. Random segregation, along with genetic recombination, accounts for the fact that while children resemble their parents, they do not look or act exactly like them. The two

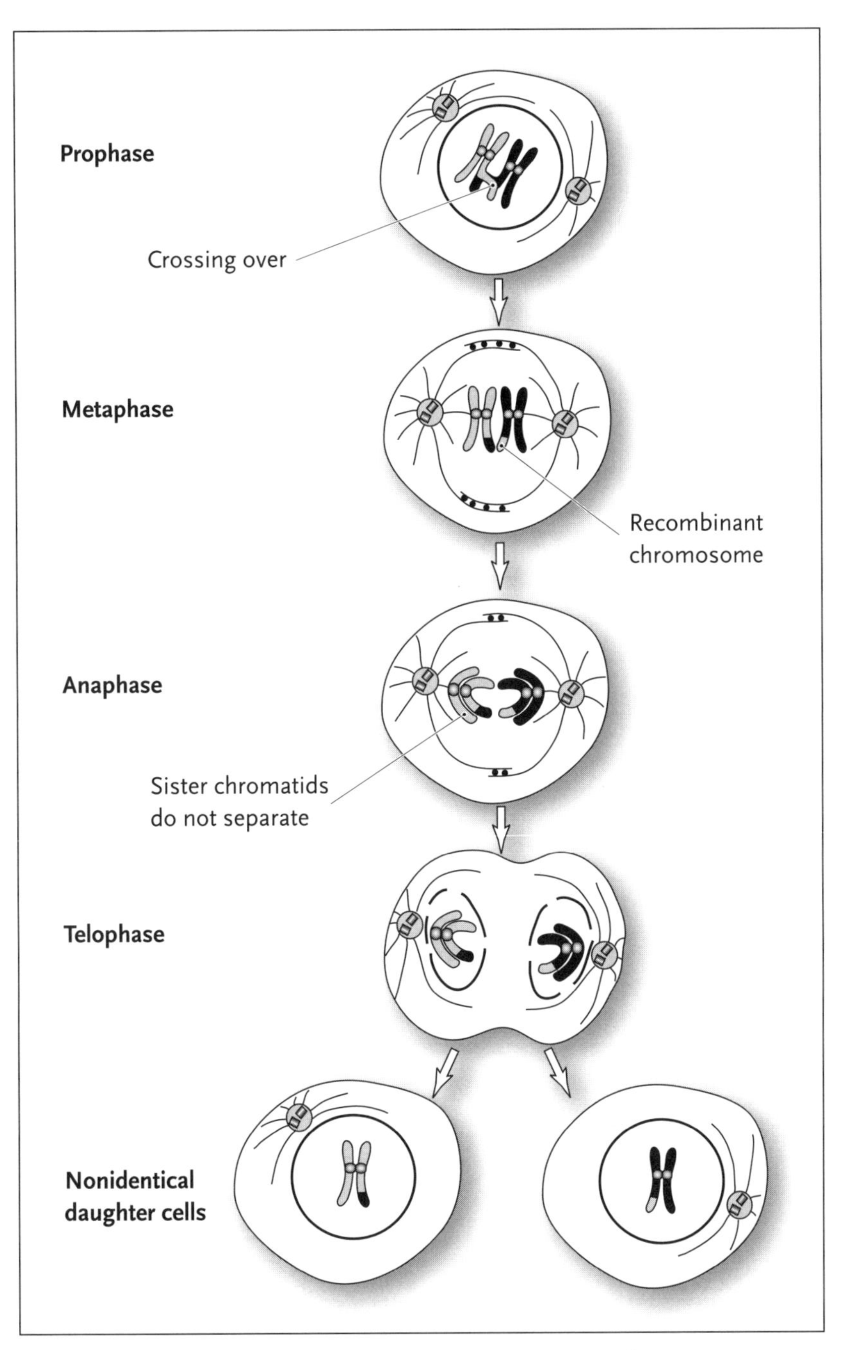

Meiosis I. The most notable features include genetic recombination (crossing over) between the homologous chromosomes during prophase, comigration of the sister chromatids during anaphase, and the production of nonidentical daughter cells. Only one homologous pair is shown.

mechanisms are responsible for the remarkable adaptability of all eukaryotes. Meiosis II begins immediately after the completion of meiosis I, which produces two daughter cells, each containing a duplicated parent chromosome and a recombinant chromosome consisting of both paternal and maternal DNA. These two cells divide mitotically to produce four haploid cells, each of which is genetically unique, containing unaltered or recombinant maternal and paternal chromosomes. Meiosis produces haploid cells by passing through two rounds of cell division with only one round of DNA synthesis. However, as we have seen, the process is not just concerned with reducing the number of chromosomes but is also involved in stirring up the genetic pot in order to produce unique gametes that may someday give rise to an equally unique individual.

DNA REPLICATION

DNA replication, which occurs during the S phase of the cell cycle, requires the coordinated effort of a team of enzymes, led by DNA helicase and primase. The helicase is a remarkable enzyme that is responsible for separating the two DNA strands, a feat that it accomplishes at an astonishing rate of 1,000 nucleotides every second. This enzyme gets its name from the fact that it unwinds the DNA helix as it separates the two strands. The enzyme that is responsible for reading the template strand and for synthesizing the new daughter strand is called DNA polymerase. This enzyme reads the parental DNA in the 3' to 5' direction and creates a daughter strand that grows 5' to 3'. DNA polymerase also has an editorial function, in that it checks the preceding nucleotide to make sure it is correct before it adds a nucleotide to the growing chain. The editor function of this enzyme introduces an interesting problem. How can the polymerase add the very first nucleotide when it has to check a preceding nucleotide before adding a new one? A special enzyme called primase, which is attached to the helicase, solves this problem. Primase synthesizes short pieces of RNA that form a DNA-RNA double-stranded region. The RNA becomes a temporary part of the daughter strand, thus priming the DNA polymerase by providing the crucial first nucleotide in the new strand. Once the chromosome is duplicated, DNA repair enzymes remove the RNA primers and replace them with DNA nucleotides.

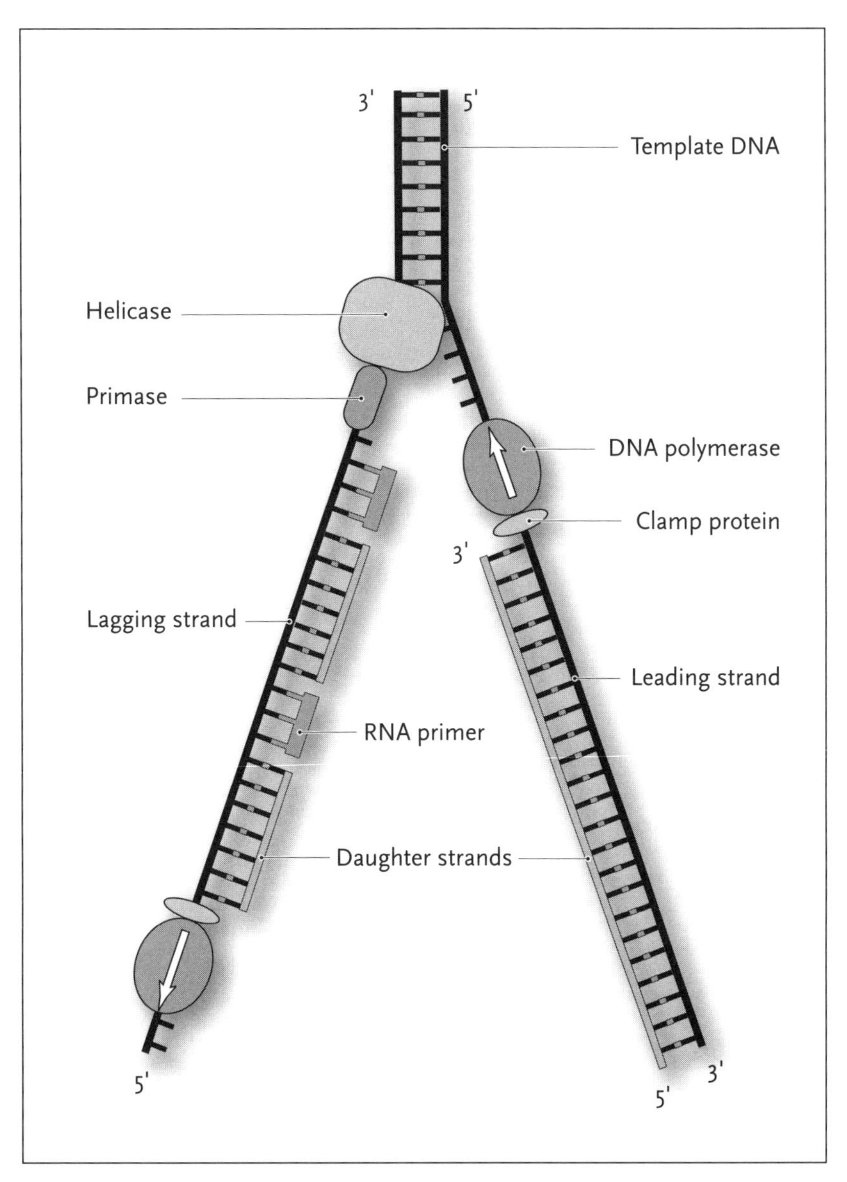

DNA replication. The helicase separates the two strands so the DNA polymerase can synthesize new strands. The primase provides replication signals for the polymerase in the form of RNA primers, and the clamp protein keeps the polymerase from falling off the DNA. The leading strand requires only a single primer (not shown). The lagging strand requires many primers, and the daughter strand is synthesized as a series of DNA fragments that are later joined into one continuous strand.

TRANSCRIPTION, TRANSLATION, AND THE GENETIC CODE

Genes encode proteins and several kinds of RNA. Extracting the information from DNA requires the processes of transcription and translation. Transcription, catalyzed by the enzyme RNA polymerase, copies one strand of the DNA into a complementary strand of messenger RNA (mRNA) or ribosomal RNA (rRNA) that is used in the construction of ribosomes. Messenger RNA translocates to the cytoplasm where it is translated into a protein by ribosomes. Newly transcribed rRNA is sent to the nucleolus for ribosome assembly, and is never translated. Ribosomes are complex structures consisting of about 50 proteins and four kinds of rRNA, known as 5S, 5.8S, 18S, and 28S rRNA (the "S" refers to a sedimentation coefficient that is proportional to size). These RNAs range in size from about 500 bases up to the 2,000 bases of the 28S. The ribosome is assembled in the nucleolus as two nonfunctional subunits before being sent out to the cytoplasm where the subunits combine, along with an mRNA, to form a fully functional unit. The production of ribosomes in this way ensures that translation never occurs in the nucleus.

The genetic code provides a way for the translation machinery to interpret the sequence information stored in the DNA molecule and represented by mRNA. DNA is a linear sequence of four different kinds of nucleotides, so the simplest code could be one in which each nucleotide specifies a different amino acid—that is, adenine coding for the amino acid glycine, cytosine for lysine, and so on. The first cells may have used this coding system, but it is limited to the construction of proteins consisting of only four different kinds of amino acids. Eventually, a more elaborate code evolved, in which a combination of three out of the four possible DNA nucleotides, called codons, specifies a single amino acid. With this scheme it is possible to have a unique code for each of the 20 naturally occurring amino acids. For example, the codon AGC specifies the amino acid serine, whereas TGC specifies the amino acid cysteine. Thus, a gene may be viewed as a long continuous sequence of codons. However, not all codons specify an amino acid. The sequence TGA signals the end of the gene, and a special codon, ATG, signals the start site, in addition to specifying the amino acid methionine. Consequently, all proteins begin with this amino acid, although it is

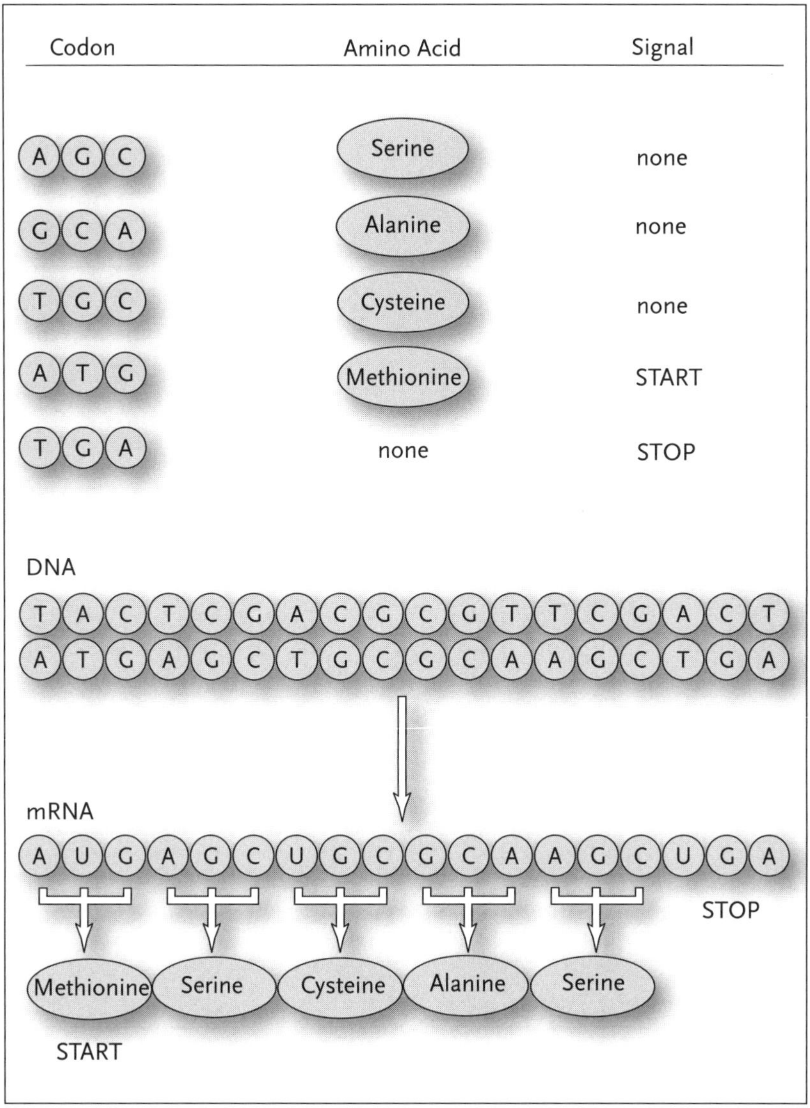
Codon
Amino Acid
Signal
A G C
Serine
none
G C A
Alanine
none
T G C
Cysteine
none
A T G
Methionine
START
T G A
none
STOP
DNA
T A C T C G A C G C G T T C G A C T
A T G A G C T G C G C A A G C T G A
mRNA
A U G A G C U G C G C A A G C U G A
STOP
Methionine
Serine
Cysteine
Alanine
Serine
START

Transcription, translation, and the genetic code. Five codons are shown, four specifying amino acids (protein subunits) and two of the five serving as start and stop signals. The codons, including the start and stop signals, are linked together to form a gene on the bottom, or coding, DNA strand. The coding strand is copied into messenger RNA (mRNA), which is used to synthesize the protein. Nucleotides appear as round beads: adenine (A), thymine (T), cytosine (C), and guanine (G). Amino acids appear as labeled elliptical beads. Note that in mRNA uracil (U) replaces the thymine (T) found in DNA.

sometimes removed once construction of the protein is complete. As mentioned above, an average protein may consist of 300 to 400 amino acids; since the codon consists of three nucleotides for each amino acid, a typical gene may be 900 to 1,200 nucleotides long.

POWER GENERATION

ATP is produced in mitochondria from AMP or ADP and phosphate (PO_4). This process involves a number of metal-binding proteins called the respiratory chain (also known as the electron transport chain), and a special ion channel–enzyme called ATP synthetase. The respiratory chain consists of three major components: NADH dehydrogenase, cytochrome b, and cytochrome oxidase. All of these components are protein complexes that have an iron (NADH dehydrogenase, cytochrome b) or a copper core (cytochrome oxidase) and, together with the ATP synthetase, are located in the inner membrane of the mitochondria. The respiratory chain is analogous to an electric cable that transports electricity from a hydroelectric dam to our homes, where it is used to turn on lights or to power our stereos. The human body, like that of all animals, generates electricity by processing food molecules through a metabolic pathway called the Krebs cycle. The electricity, or electrons so generated, travel through the respiratory chain, and as they do, they power the synthesis of ATP. All electrical circuits must have a ground, that is, the electrons need someplace to go once they have completed the circuit. In the case of the respiratory chain, the ground is oxygen. After passing through the chain, the electrons are picked up by oxygen, which combines with hydrogen ions to form water.

THE GLYCOCALYX

This structure is an enormously diverse collection of glycoproteins and glycolipids that covers the surface of every cell, like trees on the surface of the Earth, and has many important functions. All eukaryotes originated from free-living cells that hunted bacteria for food. The glycocalyx evolved to meet the demands of this kind of lifestyle, providing a way for the cell to locate, capture, and ingest food molecules or prey organisms. Cell-surface glycoproteins also form transporters and ion channels that serve as gateways into the cell. Neurons have refined ion channels for the purpose of cell-to-cell communication, giving rise to the nervous systems found in most animal species. In higher vertebrates, certain members of the glycocalyx are used by cells of the immune system as recognition markers to detect invading microbes or foreign cells introduced as an organ or tissue transplant.

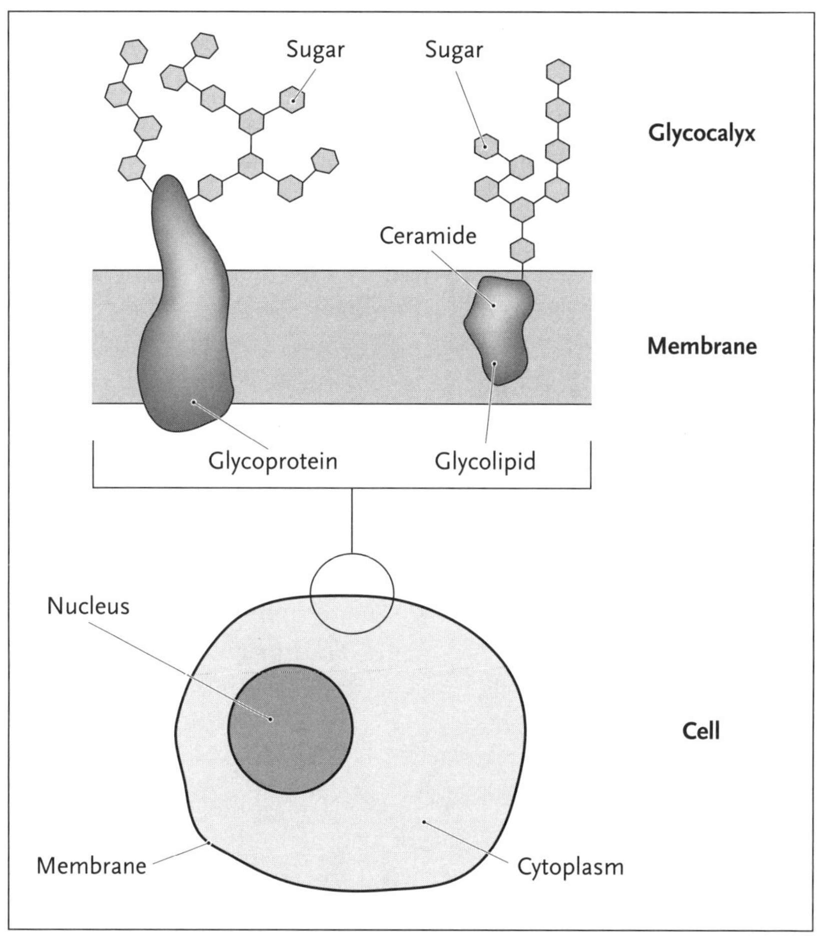

The eukaryote glycocalyx. The eukaryote's molecular forest consists of glycoproteins and glycolipids. Two examples are shown at the top, a glycoprotein on the left and a glycolipid on the right. The glycoprotein trees have "trunks" made of protein and "leaves" made of sugar molecules. Glycolipids also have "leaves" made of sugar molecules, but the "trunks" are a fatty compound called ceramide that is completely submerged within the plane of the membrane. The glycocalyx has many jobs, including cell-to-cell communication and the transport and detection of food molecules. It also provides recognition markers so the immune system can detect foreign cells.

Recombinant DNA Primer

Recombinant technology is a collection of procedures that make it possible to isolate a gene and produce enough of it for a detailed study of its structure and function. Central to this technology is the ability to construct libraries of DNA fragments that represent the genetic repertoire of an entire organism or of a specific cell type. Constructing these libraries involves splicing different pieces of DNA together to form a novel or recombinant genetic entity, from which the procedure derives its name. DNA cloning and library construction were made possible by the discovery of DNA-modifying enzymes that can seal two pieces of DNA together or can cut DNA at sequence-specific sites. Many of the procedures that are part of recombinant technology, such as DNA sequencing or filter hybridization, were developed to characterize DNA fragments that were isolated from cells or gene libraries. Obtaining the sequence of a gene has made it possible to study the organization of the genome, but more important, it has provided a simple way of determining the protein sequence and the expression profile for any gene.

DNA-MODIFYING ENZYMES

Two of the most important enzymes used in recombinant technology are those that can modify DNA by sealing two fragments together and others that can cut DNA at specific sites. The first modifying enzyme to be discovered was DNA ligase, an enzyme that can join two pieces of DNA together. It is an important component of the cell's DNA replication and repair machinery. Other DNA modifying enzymes, called restriction enzymes, cut DNA at sequence-specific sites, with different members of the family cutting at different sites. Restriction enzymes are isolated from bacteria, and since their discovery in 1970, more than 90 such enzymes have been isolated from more than 230 bacterial strains.

The name "restriction enzyme" is cryptic, and calls for an explanation. During the period when prokaryotes began to appear on Earth, their environment contained a wide assortment of molecules that were released into the soil or water by other cells, either deliberately or when the cells died. DNA of varying lengths was among these molecules, and was readily taken up by living cells. If the foreign DNA contained complete genes from a competing bacterial species, there

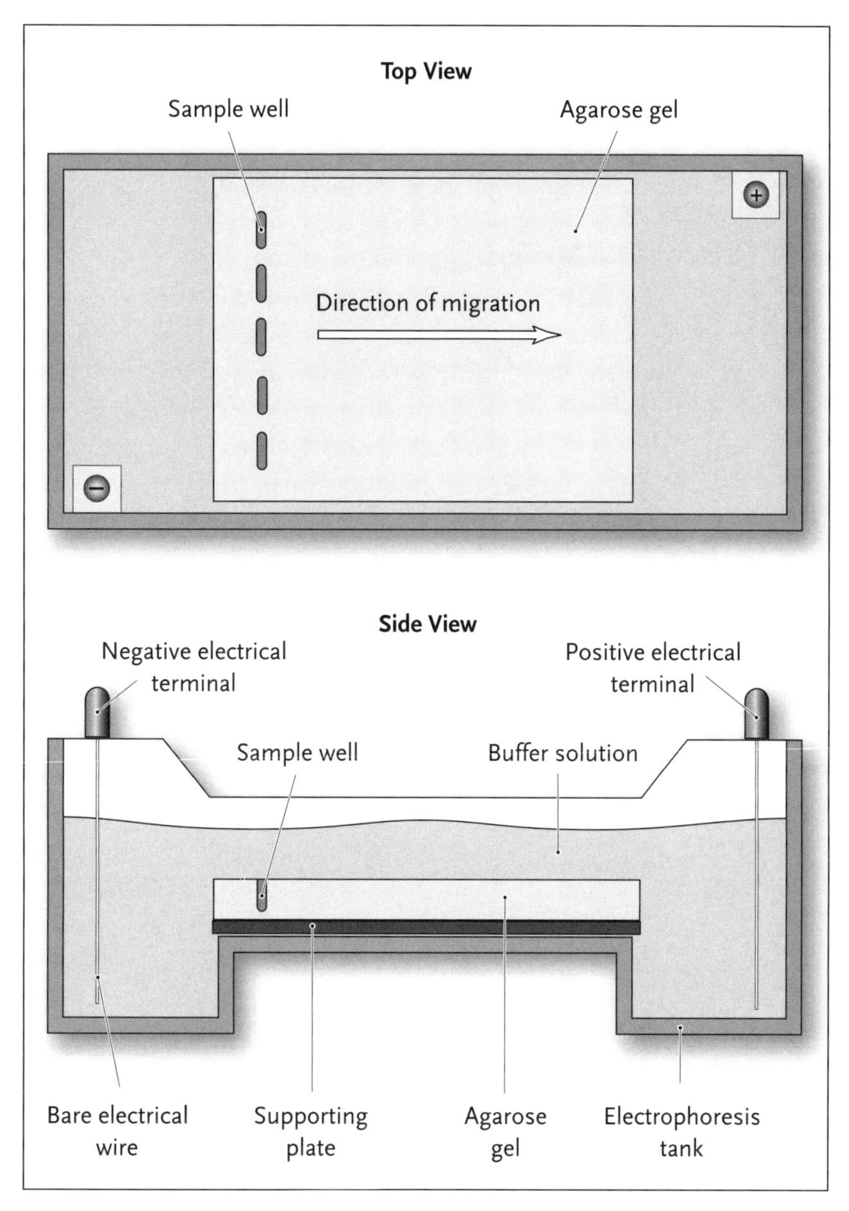

Agarose gel electrophoresis. An agarose gel is placed in an electrophoresis tank and submerged in a buffer solution. The electrical terminals are connected to a power source, with the sample wells positioned near the negative terminal. When the current is turned on, the negatively charged nucleic acids migrate towards the positive terminal. The migration rate is an inverse function of molecular size. (Large molecules travel more slowly than small ones.)

was the real possibility that those genes could have been transcribed and translated by the host cell with potentially fatal results. As a precaution, prokaryotes evolved a set of enzymes that would restrict the foreign DNA population by cutting it up into smaller pieces, before being broken down completely to individual nucleotides.

GEL ELECTROPHORESIS

This procedure is used to separate different DNA and RNA fragments in a slab of agar or polyacrylamide subjected to an electric field. Nucleic acids carry a negative charge and thus will migrate toward a positively charged electrode. The gel acts a sieving medium that impedes the movement of the molecules. Thus, the rate at which the fragments migrate is a function of their size; small fragments migrate more rapidly than large fragments. The gel, containing the sample, is submerged in a special pH-regulated solution, or buffer, containing a nucleic acid–specific dye, ethidium bromide. This dye produces a strong reddish-yellow fluorescence when exposed to untraviolet (UV) radiation. Consequently, after electrophoresis, the nucleic acid can be detected by photographing the gel under UV illumination.

DNA CLONING

In 1973 scientists discovered that restriction enzymes, DNA ligase, and bacterial plasmids could be used to clone DNA molecules. Plasmids are small (about 4,000 base pairs, also expressed as 4.0 kilo base pairs or 4 Kbp) circular minichromosomes that occur naturally in bacteria and are often exchanged between cells by passive diffusion. When a bacterium acquires a new plasmid it is said to have been transfected. For bacteria, the main advantage to swapping plasmids is that they often carry antibiotic resistance genes, so that a cell sensitive to ampicillin can become resistant simply by acquiring the right plasmid.

The first cloning experiment used a plasmid from *Escherichia coli* that was cut with the restriction enzyme *Eco*RI. The plasmid had a single *Eco*RI site, so the restriction enzyme simply opened the circular molecule, rather than cutting it up into many useless pieces. Foreign DNA, cut with the same restriction enzyme, was incubated with the plasmid. Because the plasmid and foreign DNA were both cut with *Eco*RI, the DNA could insert itself into the plasmid to form a hybrid, or recombinant plasmid, after which DNA ligase sealed the two together.

The reaction mixture was added to a small volume of *E. coli* so that some of the cells could take up the recombinant plasmid before being transferred to a nutrient broth containing streptomycin. Only those

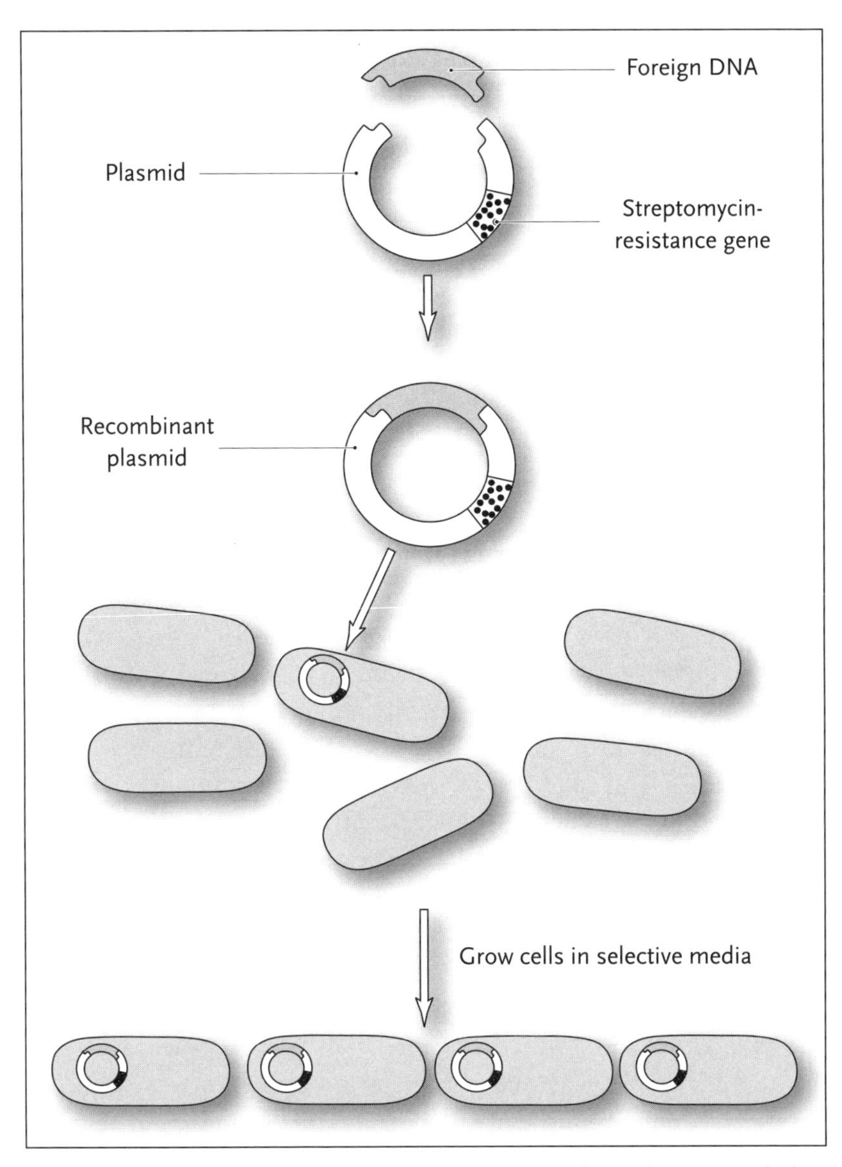

Cloning DNA in a plasmid. The foreign DNA and the plasmid are cut with the same restriction enzyme, allowed to fuse, and then sealed with DNA ligase. The recombinant plasmid is mixed with bacterial cells, some of which pick up the plasmid, allowing them to grow in a culture medium containing the antibiotic streptomycin. The bacteria's main chromosome is not shown.

cells carrying the recombinant plasmid, which contained an antistreptomycin gene, could grow in the presence of this antibiotic. Each time the cells divided, the plasmid DNA was duplicated along with the main chromosome. After the cells had grown overnight, the foreign DNA had been amplified, or cloned, billions of times and was easily isolated for sequencing or expression studies.

GENOMIC AND cDNA LIBRARIES

The basic cloning procedure described above not only provides a way to amplify a specific piece of DNA, but it can also be used to construct gene libraries. In this case, however, the cloning vector is a bacteriophage, called lambda. The lambda genome is double-stranded linear DNA of about 40 Kbp, much of which can be replaced by foreign DNA without sacrificing the ability of the virus to infect bacteria. This is the great advantage of lambda over a plasmid. Lambda can accommodate very long pieces of DNA, often long enough to contain an entire gene, whereas a plasmid cannot accommodate foreign DNA that is larger than 4 Kbp. Moreover, bacteriophage has the natural ability to infect bacteria, so that the efficiency of transfection is 100 times greater than it is for plasmids.

The construction of a gene library begins by isolating genomic DNA and digesting it with a restriction enzyme to produce fragments of 1,000 to 10,000 base pairs. These fragments are ligated into lambda genomes, which are subjected to a packaging reaction to produce mature viral particles, most of which carry a different piece of the genomic DNA. This collection of viruses is called a genomic library and is used to study the structure and organization of specific genes. Clones from such a library contain the coding sequences, in addition to introns, intervening sequences, promoters, and enhancers. An alternative form of gene library can be constructed by isolating mRNA from a specific cell type. This RNA is converted to the complimentary DNA (cDNA) using an RNA-dependent DNA polymerase called reverse transcriptase. The cDNA is ligated to lambda genomes and packaged as for the genomic library. This collection of recombinant viruses is a cDNA library and contains only genes that were being expressed by the cells when the RNA was extracted. It does not include introns or controlling elements, as these are lost during transcription and the processing that occurs in the cell to make mature mRNA. Thus a cDNA library is intended for the purpose of studying gene expression and the structure of the coding region only.

LABELING CLONED DNA

Many of the procedures used in the area of recombinant technology were inspired by the events that occur during DNA replication. This includes the labeling of cloned DNA for use as probes in expression studies, DNA sequencing, and polymerase chain reaction (PCR, described in a following section). DNA replication involves duplicating one of the strands (the parent, or template strand) by linking nucleotides in an order specified by the template, and depends on a large number of enzymes, the most important of which is DNA polymerase. This enzyme, guided by the template strand, constructs a daughter strand by linking nucleotides together. One such nucleotide is deoxyadenine triphosphate (dATP). Deoxyribonucleotides have a single hydroxyl group located at the 3' carbon of the sugar group, while the triphosphate is attached to the 5' carbon. The procedure for labeling DNA probes, developed in 1983, introduces radioactive nucleotides into a DNA molecule. This method supplies DNA polymerase with a single-stranded DNA template, a primer, and the four nucleotides in a buffered solution to induce in vitro replication. The daughter strand that becomes the probe is labeled by including a nucleotide in the reaction mix that is linked to a radioactive isotope. The radioactive nucleotide is usually deoxycytosine triphosphate (dCTP) or dATP.

Single-stranded DNA hexamers (six bases long) are used as primers, and these are produced in such a way that they contain all possible permutations of four bases taken six at a time. Randomizing the base sequence for the primers ensures that there will be at least one primer site in a template that is only 50 bp long. Templates used in labeling reactions such as this are generally 100 to 800 bp long. This strategy of labeling DNA, known as random primer or oligo labeling, is widely used in cloning and in DNA and RNA filter hybridizations (described in following sections).

DNA SEQUENCING

A sequencing reaction developed by the British biochemist Dr. Fred Sanger in 1976, DNA sequencing is another technique that takes its

Plasmid primer site for DNA sequencing. The cloned DNA is inserted into the plasmid near an engineered primer site. Once the primer binds to the primer site, the cloned DNA may be replicated, as part of a sequencing reaction, in the direction indicated by the arrow. Only one strand of the double-stranded plasmid and cloned DNA is shown.

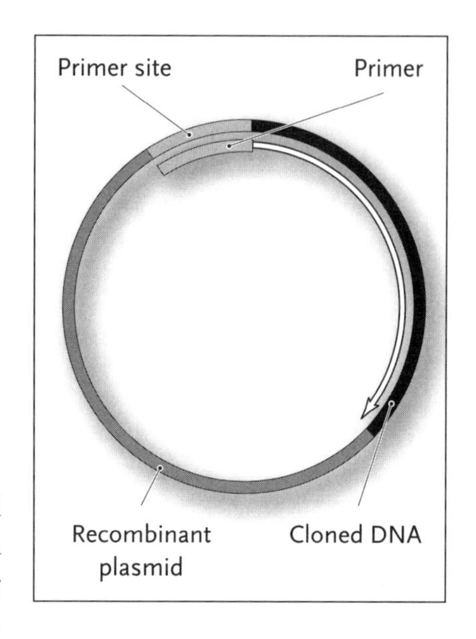

inspiration from the natural process of DNA replication. DNA polymerase requires a primer with a free 3' hydroxyl group. The polymerase adds the first nucleotide to this group, and all subsequent bases are added to the 3' hydroxyl of the previous base. Sequencing by the Sanger method is usually performed with the DNA cloned into a plasmid. This simplifies the choice of the initial primers since their sequence can be derived from the known plasmid sequence. An engineered plasmid primer site adjacent to a cloned DNA fragment is shown in the accompanying figure. Once the primer binds to the primer site the cloned DNA may be replicated. Sanger's innovation involved the synthesis of artificial nucleotides lacking the 3' hydroxyl group, thus producing dideoxynucleotides (ddATP, ddCTP, ddGTP and ddTTP). Incorporation of a dideoxynucleotide terminates the growth of the daughter strand at that point, and this can be used to determine the size of each daughter strand. The shortest daughter strand represents the complementary nucleotide at the beginning of the template, whereas the longest strand represents the complementary nucleotide at the end of the template (see table on page 103). The reaction products, consisting of all the daughter strands, are fractionated on a polyacrylamide gel. Polyacrylamide serves the same function as agarose. It has the advantage of being a tougher material, essential for the large size of a typical sequencing gel. Some of the nucleotides included in the Sanger reaction are labeled with a radioactive isotope so the fractionated daughter strands can be visualized by drying the gel and then exposing it to X-ray film. Thus, the Sanger method uses the natural process of replication to mark the position of each nucleotide in the DNA fragment so the sequence of the fragment can be determined.

A representation of a sequencing gel is shown in the accompanying figure. The sequence of the daughter strand is read beginning with the smallest fragment at the bottom of the gel, and ending with the largest fragment at the top. The sequence of the template strand (see table below) is obtained simply by taking the complement of the sequence obtained from the gel (the daughter strand).

SOUTHERN AND NORTHERN BLOTTING

One of the most important techniques to be developed, as part of recombinant technology, is the transfer of nucleic acids from an agarose gel to nylon filter paper that can be hybridized to a labeled probe to

EXAMPLE OF A SEQUENCING REACTION

Tube	Reaction Products	
A	G-C-A-T-C-G-T-C C-G-T-**A**	G-C-A-T-C-G-T-C C-G-T-A-G-C-**A**
T	G-C-A-T-C-G-T-C C-G-**T**	
C	G-C-A-T-C-G-T-C **C** G-C-A-T-C-G-T-C	G-C-A-T-C-G-T-C C-G-T-A-G-**C** G-C-A-T-C-G-T-C
G	C-**G** G-C-A-T-C-G-T-C C-G-T-A-G-C-A-**G**	C-G-T-A-**G**

The Sanger sequencing reaction is set up in four separate tubes, each containing a different di-deoxynucleotide (ddATP, ddTTP, ddCTP, and ddGTP). The reaction products are shown for each of the tubes: A (ddATP), T (ddTTP), C (ddCTP), and G (ddGTP). The template strand is GCATCGTC. Replication of the template begins after the primer binds to the primer site on the sequencing plasmid. The di-deoxynucleotide terminating the reaction is shown in bold. The daughter strands, all of different lengths, are fractionated on a polyacrylamide gel.

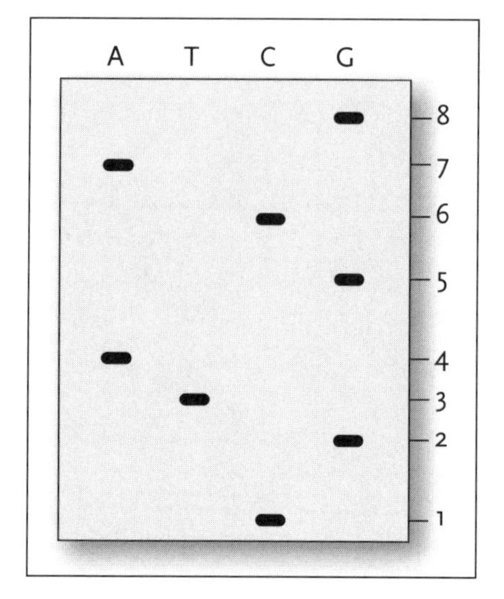

A representation of a sequencing gel. The reaction products (shown in the table on page 103) run from the top to the bottom, with the smallest fragment migrating at the highest rate. The sequence is read beginning with the smallest fragment on the gel (band no. 1, in the "C" lane) and ending with the largest fragment at the top (band no. 8, in the "G" lane). The sequence is CGTAGCAG. The complementary sequence is GCATCGTC. This is the template strand indicated in the table.

detect specific genes. This procedure was introduced by the Scottish scientist E. M. Southern in 1975 for transferring DNA and is now known as Southern blotting. Since the DNA is transferred to filter paper, the detection stage is known as filter hybridization. In 1980 the procedure was modified to transfer RNA to nylon membranes for the study of gene expression and, in reference to the original, is called northern blotting.

Northern blotting is used to study the expression of specific genes and is usually performed on messenger RNA (mRNA). Typical experiments may wish to determine the expression of specific genes in normal versus cancerous tissue, or in tissues obtained from groups of different ages. The RNA is fractionated on an agarose gel and then transferred to a nylon membrane. Paper towels placed on top of the assembly pull the transfer buffer through the gel, eluting the RNA from the gel and trapping it on the membrane. The location of specific mRNA can be determined by hybridizing the membrane to a radiolabeled cDNA or genomic clone. The hybridization procedure involves placing the filter in a buffer solution containing a labeled probe. During a long incubation period, the probe binds to the target sequence immobilized on the membrane. A-T and G-C base pairing mediate the binding between the probe and target. The double-stranded molecule that is formed is a hybrid, being formed between the RNA target, on the membrane, and the DNA probe.

FLUORESCENT IN SITU HYBRIDIZATION (FISH)

Studying gene expression does not always depend on northern blots and filter hybridization. In the 1980s scientists found that cDNA probes could be hybridized to DNA or mRNA in situ, that is, while located within cells or tissue sections fixed on microscope slides. In this case the probe is labeled with a fluorescent dye molecule, rather than a radioactive isotope. The samples are then examined and photographed under a fluorescent microscope. FISH is an extremely powerful variation on Southern and northern blots. This procedure gives precise information regarding the identity of a cell that expresses a specific gene, information that usually cannot be obtained with filter hybridization. Organs and tissues are generally composed of many different kinds of cells that cannot be separated from each other using standard biochemical extraction procedures. Histological sections, however, show clearly the various cell types, and when subjected to FISH analysis provide clear results as to which cells express specific genes. FISH is also used in clinical laboratories for the diagnosis of genetic abnormalities.

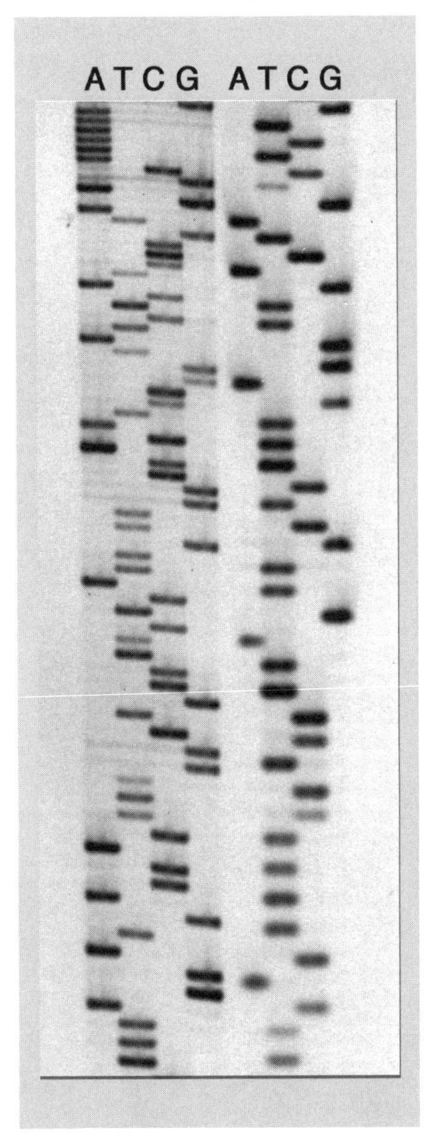

An autoradiogram of a portion of a DNA sequencing gel. A partial sequence (the first 20 bases) of the left set, beginning at the bottom of the "T" lane, is TTTAGGATGACCACTTTGGC. *(Dr. Joseph Panno)*

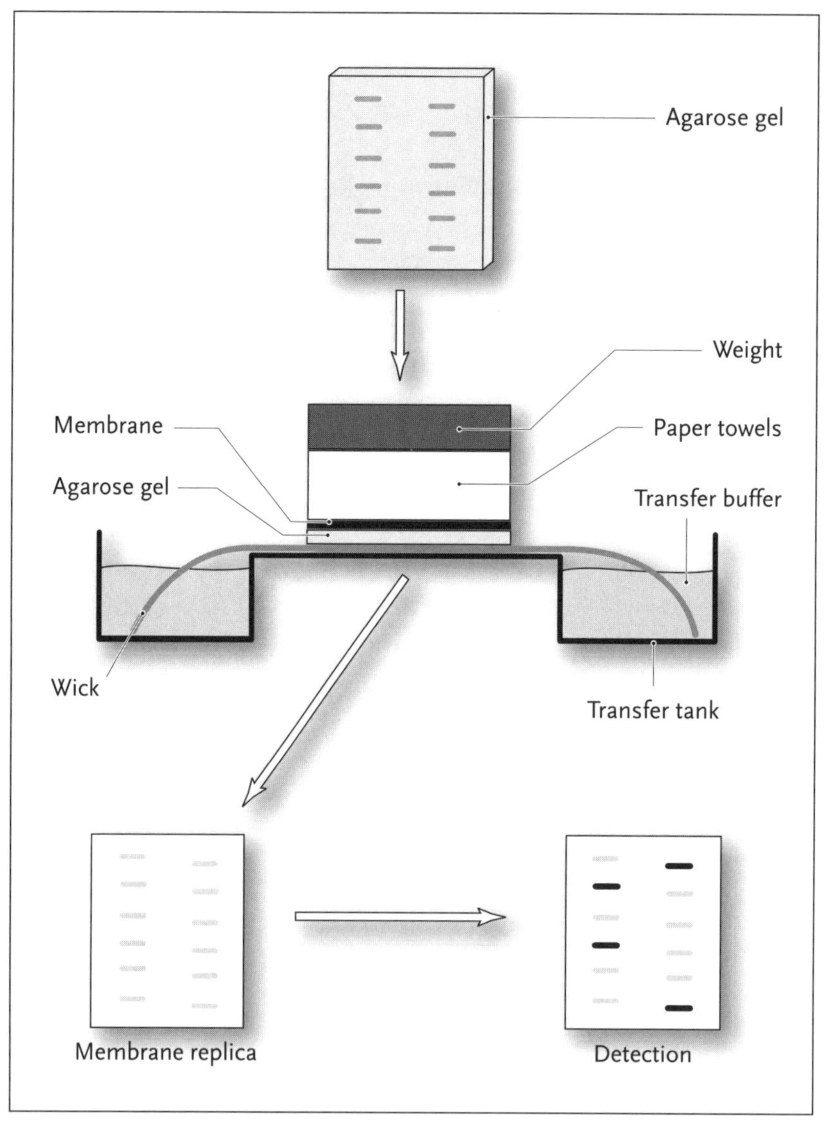

Northern transfer and membrane hybridization. RNA is fractionated on an agarose gel and then placed face down on a paper wick in a transfer tank. The gel is overlain with a piece of nylon membrane, paper towels, and weight. The paper towels draw the buffer through the gel and the membrane. A flow of buffer elutes the RNA from the gel, transferring it to the membrane. A radiolabeled cDNA probe is hybridized to the membrane to detect specific mRNA transcripts. Note that the thickness of the membrane is exaggerated for clarity.

POLYMERASE CHAIN REACTION (PCR)

PCR is simply repetitive DNA replication over a limited, primer defined, region of a suitable template. The region defined by the primers is amplified to such an extent that it can be easily isolated for further study. The reaction exploits the fact that a DNA duplex, in a low salt buffer, will melt (that is, separate into two single strands) at 75°C, but will reanneal (rehybridize) at 37°C. The reaction is initiated by melting the template, in the presence of primers and polymerase in a suitable buffer, cooling quickly to 37°C, and allowing sufficient time for the polymerase to replicate both strands of the template. The temperature is then increased to 75°C to melt the newly formed duplexes and then cooled to 37°C. At the lower temperature more primer will anneal to initiate another round of replication. The heating-cooling cycle is repeated 20 to 30 times, after which the reaction products are fractionated on an agarose gel and photographed. The band containing the amplified fragment may be cut out of the gel and purified for further study. The DNA polymerase used in these reactions is isolated from thermophilic bacteria that can withstand temperatures of 70°C to 80°C. PCR applications are nearly limitless. It is used to amplify DNA from samples containing, at times, no more than a few cells. It can be used to screen libraries and to identify genes that are turned on or off during embryonic development or during cellular transformation.

Gene Therapy Primer

When we get sick it often is due to invading microbes that destroy or damage cells and organs in our body. Cholera, smallpox, measles, diphtheria, AIDS, and the common cold are all examples of what we call an infectious disease. If we catch any of these diseases, our doctor may prescribe a drug that will, in some cases, remove the microbe from our bodies, thus curing the disease. Unfortunately, most of the diseases that we fall prey to are not of the infectious kind. In such case, there are no microbes to fight, no drugs to apply. Instead, we are faced with a far more difficult problem, for this type of disease is an ailment that damages a gene. Gene therapy attempts to cure these diseases by replacing or supplementing the damaged gene.

When a gene is damaged, it usually is caused by a point mutation, a change that affects a single nucleotide. Sickle-cell anemia, a disease affecting red blood cells, was the first genetic disorder of this kind to be described. The mutation occurs in a gene that codes for the β (beta) chain of hemoglobin, converting the codon GAG to GTG, which

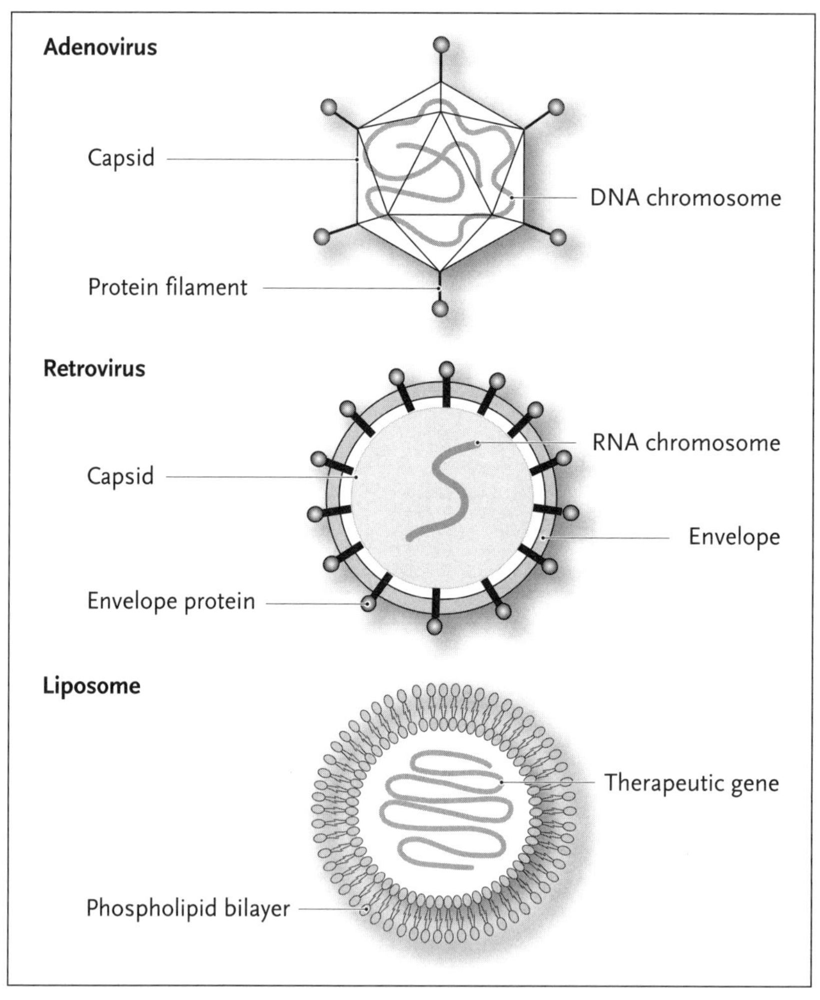

Vectors used in gene therapy. Adenoviruses have a DNA genome contained in a crystalline protein capsid, and normally infect cells of the upper respiratory tract, causing colds and flulike symptoms. The protein filaments are used to infect cells. Retroviruses have an RNA genome that is converted to DNA when a cell is infected. The capsid is enclosed in a phospholipid envelope, studded with proteins that are used to infect cells. The HIV (AIDS) virus is a common example of a retrovirus. Artificial vectors have also been used, consisting of a phospholipid bilayer enclosing the therapeutic gene.

substitutes the amino acid valine at position 6, for glutamic acid. This single amino-acid substitution is enough to cripple the hemoglobin molecule, making it impossible for it to carry enough oxygen to meet the demands of a normal adult. Scientists have identified several thousand genetic disorders that are known to be responsible for diseases such as breast cancer, colon cancer, hemophilia, and two neurological disorders, Alzheimer's disease and Parkinson's disease.

Gene therapy is made possible by recombinant DNA technology (biotechnology). Central to this technology is the use of viruses to clone specific pieces of DNA. That is, the DNA is inserted into a viral chromosome and is amplified as the virus multiplies. Viruses are parasites that specialize in infecting bacterial and animal cells. Consequently, scientists realized that a therapeutic gene could be inserted into a patient's cells by first introducing it into a virus and then letting the virus carry it into the affected cells. In this context the virus is referred to as the gene therapy delivery vehicle or vector (in recombinant technology it is referred to as a cloning vector).

Commonly used viruses are the retrovirus and the adenovirus. A retrovirus gets its name from the fact that it has an RNA genome that is copied into DNA after it infects a cell. Coronaviruses (cause of the common cold) and the AIDS virus are common examples of retroviruses. The adenovirus (from adenoid, the gland from which the virus was first isolated) normally infects the upper respiratory tract, causing colds and flulike symptoms. This virus, unlike the retrovirus, has a DNA genome. Artificial vectors called liposomes have also been used that consist of a phospholipid vesicle (bubble) containing the therapeutic gene.

Gene therapy vectors are prepared by cutting the viral chromosome and the therapeutic gene with the same restriction enzyme, after which the two are joined together with a DNA ligase. This recombinant chromosome is packaged into viral particles to form the final vector. The vector may be introduced into cultured cells suffering from a genetic defect, and then returned to the patient from whom they were derived (ex vivo delivery). Alternatively, the vector may be injected directly into the patient's circulatory system (in vivo delivery). The ex vivo procedure is used when the genetic defect appears in white blood cells or in stem cells that may be harvested from the patient and grown in culture.

Vector preparation and delivery. A viral chromosome and a therapeutic gene are cut with the same restriction enzyme and joined together, after which the recombinant chromosome is packaged into viral particles to form the vector. The vector may be introduced into cultured cells and then returned to the patient from whom they were derived (*ex vivo* delivery), or the vector may be injected directly into the patient's circulatory system (*in vivo* delivery).

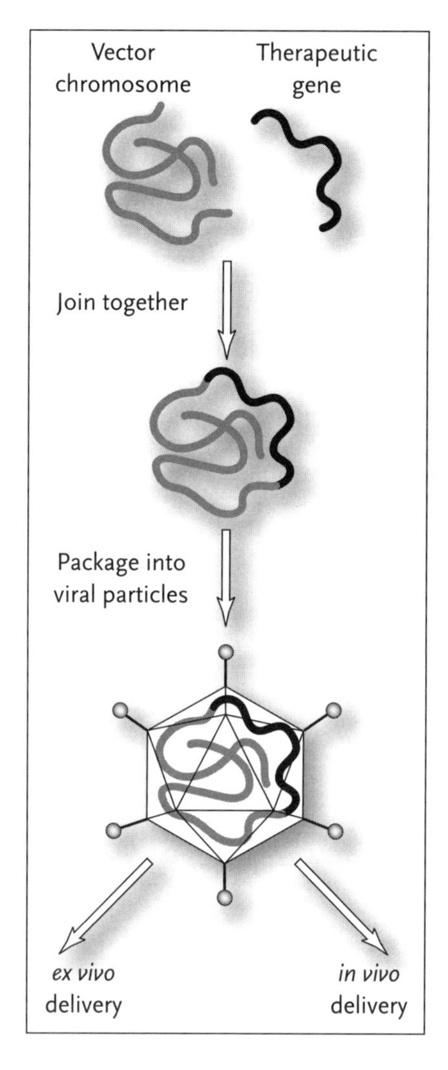

The in vivo procedure is used when the genetic defect appears in an organ, such as the liver, brain, or pancreas. This is the most common form of gene therapy, but it is also potentially hazardous, because vectors, being free in the circulatory system, may infect a wide range of cells, thus activating an immune response that could lead to widespread tissue and organ damage.

The first gene therapy trial, conducted in 1990, used ex vivo delivery. This trial cured a young patient named Ashi DeSilva of an immune deficiency (adenosine deaminase deficiency) that affects white blood cells. Other trials since then have either been ineffective or were devastating failures. Such a case occurred in 1999, when Jesse Gelsinger, an 18-year-old patient suffering from a liver disease, died while participating in a gene therapy trial. His death was caused by multiorgan failure brought on by the viral vector. In 2002 two children being treated for another form of immune deficiency developed vector-induced leukemia (cancer of the white blood cells). Despite these setbacks, gene therapy holds great promise as a medical therapy, and there are currently more than 600 trials in progress in the United States alone to treat a variety of genetic disorders.

Matching Tissues

A molecular forest called the glycocalyx covers the surface of every cell and has a central role in the process of matching tissues for transplant operations. The glycocalyx consists of a diverse population of treelike glycoproteins and glycolipids that have "trunks" made of protein, or lipid, and "leaves" made of sugar. These molecular trees are embedded in the cell membrane much like the trees of Earth are rooted in the soil (see the figure on page 112). A panoramic view of the glycocalyx, consisting of different kinds of glycoproteins and glycolipids, enhances the impression of a surrealistic forested landscape.

The exact composition of the glycocalyx varies with each individual, much in the way that an Earth forest located at the equator is different from one located in the Northern Hemisphere. The human immune system uses the spatial arrangement of the exposed sugar groups to decide whether a cell is foreign or not. Thus the glycocalyx is like a cell's fingerprint, and if that fingerprint does not pass the recognition test, the cell is destroyed, or forced to commit suicide. Immunologists refer to the glycoproteins and glycolipids in the glycocalyx as cell-surface antigens. The term *antigen* derives from the fact that cell-surface glycoproteins on a foreign cell can generate a response from the immune system that leads to the production of antibodies capable of binding to and destroying the foreign cell.

An extremely important pair of cell-surface glycolipids is known as the A and B antigens. These glycolipids occur on the surface of red blood cells and form the ABO blood group system that determines each individual's basic blood type. The A and B antigens are derived from a third antigen called H, which all individuals possess. Blood type A is produced by the *A* gene, which codes for a glycosyl transferase that adds an N-acetylgalactosamine to the H antigen. Blood type B is produced by a different transferase that places a galactose molecule on the H antigen. Some individuals have both A and B transferases and thus are said to have blood type AB. Individuals with blood type O have neither transferase. In North America, blood types A and O dominate, with A occurring in 41 percent of the population and O in 45 percent. Blood types B and AB are rare, with B occurring at a frequency of 10 percent and AB at only 4 percent.

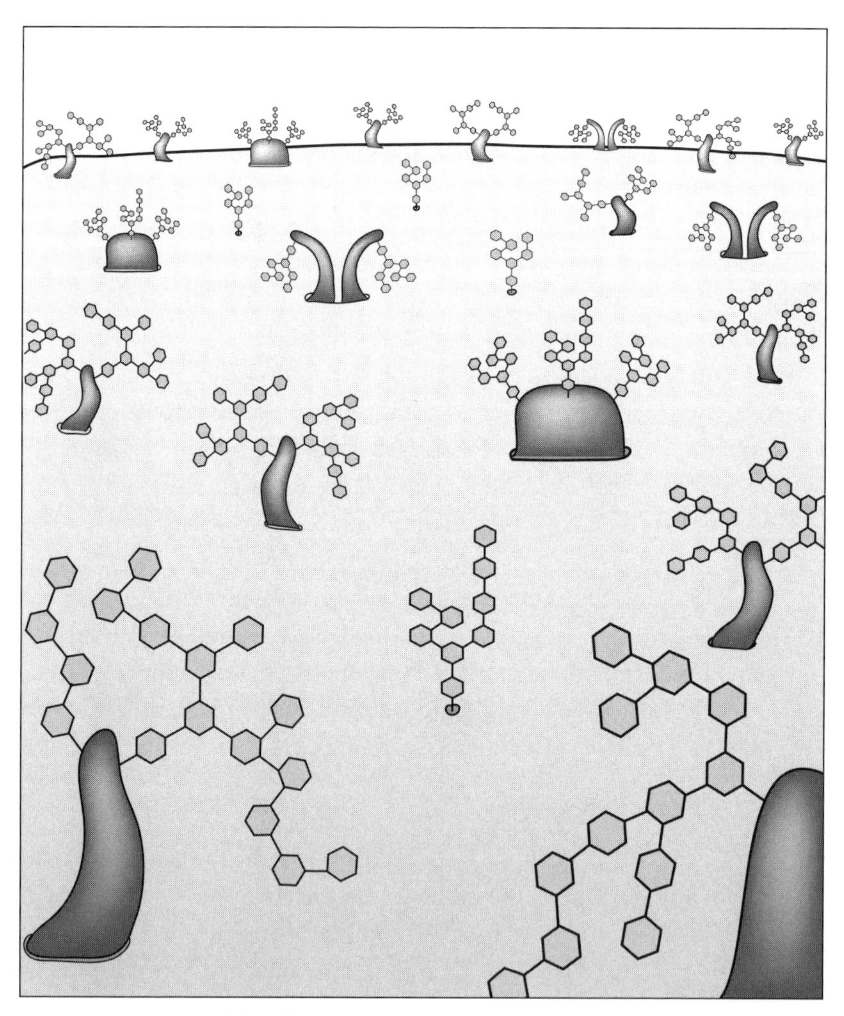

A panoramic view of the glycocalyx. The glycoproteins in the cell's forest come in many different shapes and sizes, and they dominate the surface of most cells. The glycolipids all have the same ceramide trunks, but the molecular foliage varies considerably. All but four of the structures in this image are glycoproteins.

An individual that is blood type A will form antibodies against the B antigen, and therefore cannot receive blood from a type B individual, but can receive blood from type O individuals. Similarly, a type B individual cannot receive blood from someone with blood type A, but can receive it from someone that is type O. Individuals that have blood type AB can receive blood from individuals that have blood types A, B, or O, and therefore such individuals are called universal recipients. On the other hand, people with blood type O can only receive type O blood since they will form antibodies against both A and B antigens. While individuals with type AB blood are universal recipients, individuals with type O blood are called universal donors, because their blood may be given to anyone without fear of invoking an immune response.

The importance of blood type with respect to organ transplantation is best illustrated by the recent case of Jesica Santillan, a 17-year-old girl who required a heart-lung transplant to correct a congenital lung defect that also damaged her heart. On February 7, 2003, physicians at Duke University Hospital in Durham, North Carolina, replaced Jesica's heart and lungs without checking the blood type of the donor. Jesica was blood type O, but the donor was type A. Jesica's immune system rejected the mismatched organs and she lapsed into a deep coma soon after the operation was completed. In a desperate attempt to correct the mistake, Jesica's surgeons replaced the mismatched heart and lungs with organs obtained from a type O donor, but it was too late. Jesica had already suffered severe and irreparable brain damage, and on February 22, 2003, she died.

The A and B antigens, as critically important as they are to the success of transplant surgery, are only two of many thousands of cell-surface antigens that play a role in the rejection of foreign tissue. A second major group of antigens, called the human leukocyte antigens (HLA), may in fact number in the millions. These antigens are glycoproteins that cover the surface of virtually every cell in the body; they are called leukocyte antigens simply because leukocytes were the cells from which they were originally identified. When faced with this level of complexity, transplant surgeons have had to content themselves with matching only five or six of the most common HLA antigens between the recipient and donor. This, of course, leaves many mismatched antigens, but it seems that some antigens elicit a much stronger immune response than others, an effect that is likely quantitative in nature. That is, a million copies of antigen X will catch the attention of the immune system much more effectively than will 10 copies of antigen Y. By matching the dominant antigens, surgeons hope to avoid what is called the hyperacute immune response, which leads to the immediate destruction of the transplanted organ and death of the patient. It was a hyperacute response brought on by a mismatch of dominant antigens that killed Jesica Santillan. Matching dominant antigens does not mean the transplanted organ is compatible,

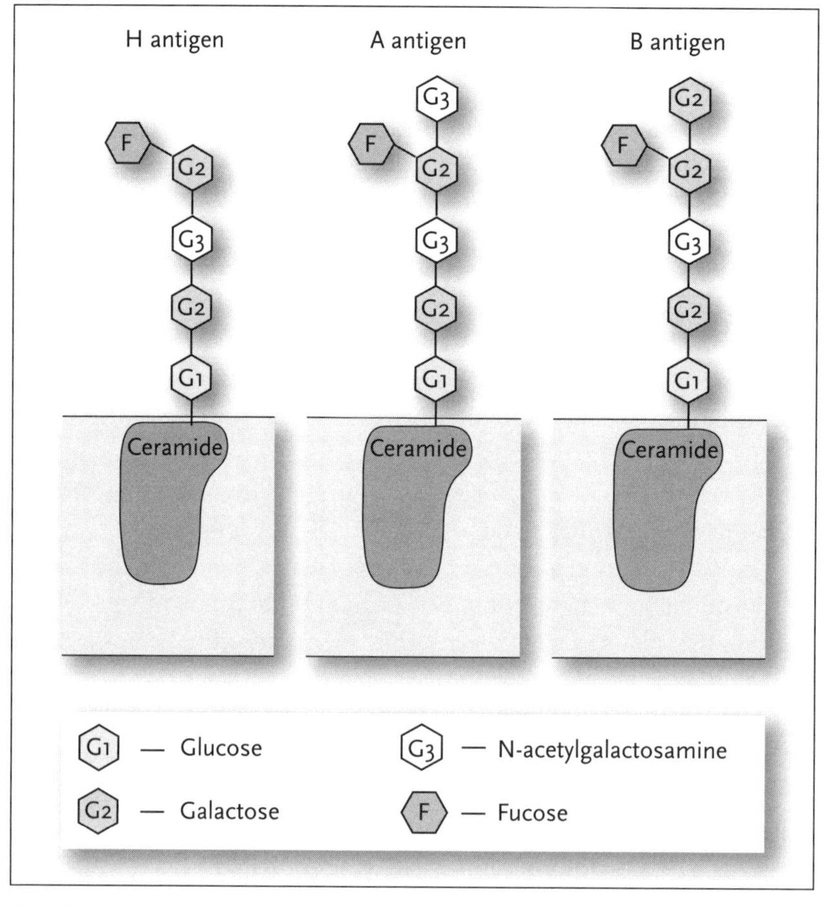

The ABO antigens on the surface of red blood cells. All individuals have the H antigen. In addition, 41 percent of North Americans have the A antigen, 10 percent have B, 4 percent have both A and B, and 45 percent have neither. The latter group is said to be type O.

but only that the patient has a good chance of surviving the first year. Beyond that, the immune system begins a slow, chronic attack on the remaining mismatched antigens, leading to eventual failure of most transplanted organs. The slow chronic attack is responsible for the poor five- and 10-year survival of transplant patients.

The Human Genome Project

Sequencing the entire human genome is an idea that grew over a period of 20 years, beginning in the early 1980s. At that time, the DNA sequencing method invented by the British biochemist Fred Sanger, then at the University of Cambridge, was but a few years old and had only been used to sequence viral or mitochondrial genomes. (See chapter 8 for a description of sequencing methods.) Indeed, one of the first genomes to be sequenced was that of bacteriophage G4, a virus that infects the bacterium *E. coli.* The G4 genome consists of 5,577 nucleotide pairs (or base pairs, abbreviated bp) and was sequenced in Dr. Sanger's laboratory in 1979. By 1982 the Sanger protocol was used by others to sequence the genome of the animal virus SV40 (5,224 bp), the human mitochondrion (16,569 bp), and bacteriophage lambda (48,502 bp). Besides providing invaluable data, these projects demonstrated the feasibility of sequencing very large genomes.

The possibility of sequencing the entire human genome was first discussed at scientific meetings organized by the U.S. Department of Energy (DOE) between 1984 and 1986. A committee appointed by the U.S. National Research Council endorsed the idea in 1988 but recommended a broader program to include the sequencing of the genes of humans, bacteria, yeast, worms, flies, and mice. They also called for the establishment of research programs devoted to the ethical, legal, and social issues raised by human genome research. The program was formally launched in late 1900 as a consortium consisting of coordinated sequencing projects in the United States, Britain, France, Germany, Japan, and China. At about the same time, the Human Genome Organization (HUGO) was founded to provide a forum for international coordination of genomic research.

By 1995 the consortium had established a strategy called hierarchical shotgun sequencing that they applied to the human genome as well as to the other organisms mentioned. With this strategy, genomic DNA is cut into one-megabase (Mb) fragments (that is, each fragment consists of 1 million bases) that are cloned into bacterial artificial chromosomes (BACs) to form a library of DNA fragments. The BAC fragments are partially characterized, then organized into an overlapping assembly called a contig. Clones are selected from the contigs for shotgun sequencing. That is, each shotgun clone is digested into small 1,000 bp fragments, sequenced, and then assembled into the final sequence with the aid of computers. Organizing the initial BAC fragments into contigs greatly simplifies the final assembly stage.

Sequencing of the human genome was divided into two stages. The first stage, completed in 2001, was a rough draft that covered about 80 percent of the genome with an estimated size of more than 3 billion bases (also expressed as 3 gigabases, or 3 Gb). The final draft, completed in April 2003, covers the entire genome and refines the data for areas of the genome that were difficult to sequence. It also filled in many gaps that were present in the rough draft. The final draft of the human genome gives us a great deal of information that may be divided into three categories: gene content, gene origins, and gene organization.

GENE CONTENT

Analysis of the final draft has shown that the human genome consists of 3.2 Gb of DNA, which encodes about 30,000 genes (estimates range between 25,000 and 32,000). The estimated number of genes is surprisingly low; many scientists had believed the human genome contained 100,000 genes. By comparison, the fruit fly, *Drosophila,* has 13,338 genes, and the simple roundworm, *Caenorhabditis elegans,* has 18,266. The genome data suggests that human complexity, as compared to the fruit fly or the worm, is not simply due to the absolute number of genes, but involves the complexity of the proteins that are encoded by those genes. In general, human proteins tend to be much more complex than those of lower organisms. Data from the final draft and other sources provides a detailed overview of the functional profile of human cellular proteins.

GENE ORIGINS

Fully one-half of human genes originated as transposable elements, also known as jumping genes. Equally surprising is the fact that 220 of our genes were obtained by horizontal transfer from bacteria, rather than ancestral, or vertical, inheritance. In other words, we obtained these genes directly from bacteria, probably during episodes of infection, in a kind of natural gene therapy, or gene swapping. We know this to be the case because while these genes occur in bacteria they are not present in yeast, fruit flies, or any other eukaryotes that have been tested.

The function of most of the horizontally tranferred genes is unclear, although a few may code for basic metabolic enzymes. A notable exception is a gene that codes for an enzyme called monoamine oxidase (MAO). Monoamines are neurotransmitters, such as dopamine, norepinephrine, and serotonin, which are needed for neural signaling in the human central nervous system. Monoamine oxidase plays a crucial role in the turnover of these neurotransmitters. How MAO, obtained from bacteria, could have developed such an important role in human physiology is a great mystery.

GENE ORGANIZATION

In prokaryotes, genes are simply arranged in tandem along the chromosome, with little, if any, DNA separating one gene from the other. Each gene is transcribed into messenger RNA (mRNA), which is translated into protein. Indeed, in prokaryotes, which have no nucleus, translation often begins even before transcription is complete. In eukaryotes, as we might expect, gene organization is more complex. Data from the genome project shows clearly that eukaryote genes are split into subunits called exons, and that each exon is separated by a length of DNA called an intron. A gene consisting of introns and exons is separated from other genes by long stretches of noncoding DNA called intervening sequences. Eukaryote genes are transcribed into a primary RNA molecule that includes exon and intron sequences. The primary transcript never leaves the nucleus and is never translated into protein. Nuclear enzymes remove the introns from the primary transcript, after which the exons are joined together to form the mature mRNA. Thus, only the exons carry the necessary code to produce a protein.

GLOSSARY

acetyl A chemical group derived from acetic acid. Important in energy metabolism and for the modification of proteins.

acetylcholine A neurotransmitter released at axonal terminals by cholinergic neurons. Found in the central and peripheral nervous system and released at the vertebrate neuromuscular junction.

acetyl-CoA A water-soluble molecule, coenzyme A (CoA), that carries acetyl groups in cells.

acid A substance that releases protons when dissolved in water. Carries a net negative charge.

actin filament A protein filament formed by the polymerization of globular actin molecules. Forms the cytoskeleton of all eukaryotes and part of the contractile apparatus of skeletal muscle.

action potential A self-propagating electrical impulse that occurs in the membranes of neurons, muscles, photoreceptors, and hair cells of the inner ear.

active transport Movement of molecules across the cell membrane, utilizing the energy stored in ATP.

adenylate cyclase A membrane-bound enzyme that catalyzes the conversion of ATP to cyclic AMP. An important component of cell-signaling pathways.

adherens junction A cell junction in which the cytoplasmic face of the membrane is attached to actin filaments.

adipocyte A fat cell.

adrenaline (epinephrine) A hormone released by chromaffin cells in the adrenal gland. Prepares an animal for extreme activity, increases the heart rate and blood-sugar levels.

adult stem cells Stem cells isolated from adult tissues, such as bone marrow or epithelium.

aerobic Refers to a process that either requires oxygen or occurs in its presence.

allele An alternate form of a gene. Diploid organisms have two alleles for each gene, located at the same locus (position) on homologous chromosomes.

allogeneic transplant A patient receives a tissue or organ transplant from an unrelated individual.

alpha helix A common folding pattern of proteins in which a linear sequence of amino acids twists into a right-handed helix stabilized by hydrogen bonds.

amino acid An organic molecule containing amino and carboxyl groups that is a building block of protein.

aminoacyl-tRNA An amino acid linked by its carboxyl group to a hydroxyl group on tRNA.

aminoacyl-tRNA synthetase An enzyme that attaches the correct amino acid to a tRNA.

amino terminus The end of a protein or polypeptide chain that carries a free amino group.

amphipathic Having both hydrophilic and hydrophobic regions, as in a phospholipid.

anabolism A collection of metabolic reactions in a cell whereby large molecules are made from smaller ones.

anaerobic A cellular metabolism that does not depend on molecular oxygen.

anaphase A mitotic stage in which the two sets of chromosomes move away from each other toward opposite and spindle poles.

anchoring junction A cell junction that attaches cells to each other.

angiogenesis Sprouting of new blood vessels from preexisting ones.

angstrom A unit of length, equal to 10^{-10} meter or 0.1 nanometer (nm), that is used to measure molecules and atoms.

anterior A position close to or at the head end of the body.

antibiotic A substance made by bacteria, fungi, and plants that is toxic to microorganisms. Common examples are penicillin and streptomycin.

antibody A protein made by B cells of the immune system in response to invading microbes.

anticodon A sequence of three nucleotides in tRNA that is complementary to a messenger RNA codon.

antigen A molecule that stimulates an immune response, leading to the formation of antibodies.

antigen-presenting cell A cell of the immune system, such as a monocyte, that presents pieces of an invading microbe (the antigen) to lymphocytes.

antiparallel The relative orientation of the two strands in a DNA double helix; the polarity of one strand is oriented in the opposite direction to the other.

antiporter A membrane carrier protein that transports two different molecules across a membrane in opposite directions.

apoptosis Regulated or programmed form of cell death that may be activated by the cell itself or by the immune system to force cells to commit suicide when they become infected with a virus.

asexual reproduction The process of forming new individuals without gametes or the fertilization of an egg by a sperm. Individuals produced this way are identical to the parent and referred to as a clone.

aster The star-shaped arrangement of microtubules that is characteristic of a mitotic or meiotic spindle.

ATP (adenosine triphosphate) A nucleoside consisting of adenine, ribose, and three phosphate groups that is the main carrier of chemical energy in the cell.

ATPase Any enzyme that catalyzes a biochemical reaction by extracting the necessary energy from ATP.

ATP synthase A protein located in the inner membrane of the mitochondrion that catalyzes the formation of ATP from ADP and inorganic phosphate using the energy supplied by the electron transport chain.

autogeneic transplant A patient receives a transplant of his or her own tissue.

autosome Any chromosome other than a sex chromosome.

axon A long extension of a neuron's cell body that transmits an electrical signal to other neurons.

axonal transport The transport of organelles, such as Golgi vesicles, along an axon to the axonal terminus. Transport also flows from the terminus to the cell body.

bacteria One of the most ancient forms of cellular life (the other is the Archaea). Bacteria are prokaryotes and some are known to cause disease.

bacterial artificial chromosome (BAC) A cloning vector that accommodates DNA inserts of up to 1 million base pairs.

bacteriophage A virus that infects bacteria. Bacteriophages were used to prove that DNA is the cell's genetic material and are now used as cloning vectors.

base A substance that can accept a proton in solution. The purines and pyrimidines in DNA and RNA are organic bases and are often referred to simply as bases.

base pair Two nucleotides in RNA or DNA that are held together by hydrogen bonds. Adenine bound to thymine or guanine bound to cytosine are examples of base pairs.

B cell (B lymphocyte) A white blood cell that makes antibodies and is part of the adaptive immune response.

benign Tumors that grow to a limited size and do not spread to other parts of the body.

beta sheet Common structural motif in proteins in which different strands of the protein run alongside each other and are held together by hydrogen bonds.

biopsy The removal of cells or tissues for examination under a microscope. When only a sample of tissue is removed, the procedure is called an incisional biopsy or core biopsy. When an entire lump or suspicious area is removed, the procedure is called an excisional biopsy. When a sample of tissue or fluid is removed with a needle, the procedure is called a needle biopsy or fine-needle aspiration.

biosphere The world of living organisms.

bivalent A duplicated chromosome paired with its homologous duplicated chromosome at the beginning of meiosis.

blastomere A cell formed by the cleavage of a fertilized egg. Blastomeres are the totipotent cells of the early embryo.

blotting A technique for transferring DNA (Southern blotting), RNA (northern blotting), or proteins (western blotting) from an agarose or polyacrylamide gel to a nylon membrane.

BRCA1 (breast cancer gene 1) A gene on chromosome 17 that may be involved in regulating the cell cycle. A person who inherits an altered version of the BRCA1 gene has a higher risk of getting breast, ovarian, or prostate cancer.

BRCA2 (breast cancer gene 2) A gene on chromosome 13 that, when mutated, increases the risk of getting breast, ovarian, or prostate cancer.

budding yeast The common name for the baker's yeast *Saccharomyces cerevisiae,* a popular experimental organism that reproduces by budding off a parental cell.

cadherin Belongs to a family of proteins that mediates cell-to-cell adhesion in animal tissues.

calorie A unit of heat. One calorie is the amount of heat needed to raise the temperature of one gram of water by 1°C. Kilocalories (1,000 calories) are used to describe the energy content of foods.

capsid The protein coat of a virus, formed by auto-assembly of one or more proteins into a geometrically symmetrical structure.

carbohydrate A general class of compounds that includes sugars, containing carbon, hydrogen, and oxygen.

carboxyl group A carbon atom attached to an oxygen and a hydroxyl group.

carboxyl terminus The end of a protein containing a carboxyl group.

carcinogen A compound or form of radiation that can cause cancer.

carcinogenesis The formation of a cancer.

carcinoma Cancer of the epithelium, representing the majority of human cancers.

cardiac muscle Muscle of the heart. Composed of myocytes that are linked together in a communication network based on free passage of small molecules through gap junctions.

caspase A protease involved in the initiation of apoptosis.

catabolism Enzyme-regulated breakdown of large molecules for the extraction of chemical-bond energy. Intermediate products are called catabolites.

catalyst A substance that lowers the activation energy of a reaction.

CD28 Cell-surface protein located in T cell membranes, necessary for the activation of T cells by foreign antigens.

cDNA (complementary DNA) DNA that is synthesized from mRNA, thus containing the complementary sequence. cDNA contains coding sequence but not the regulatory sequences that are present in the genome. Labeled probes are made from cDNA for the study of gene expression.

cell adhesion molecule (CAM) A cell surface protein that is used to connect cells to each other.

cell body The main part of a cell containing the nucleus, Golgi complex, and endoplasmic reticulum. Used in reference to neurons that have long processes (dendrites and axons) extending some distance from the nucleus and cytoplasmic machinery.

cell coat See **glycocalyx**.

cell-cycle control system A team of regulatory proteins that governs progression through the cell cycle.

cell-division-cycle gene (*cdc* gene) A gene that controls a specific step in the cell cycle.

cell fate The final differentiated state that a pluripotent embryonic cell is expected to attain.

cell-medicated immune response Activation of specific cells to launch an immune response against an invading microbe.

cell nuclear replacement Animal-cloning technique whereby a somatic cell nucleus is transferred to an enucleated oocyte. Synonomous with somatic-cell nuclear transfer.

central nervous system (CNS) That part of a nervous system that analyzes signals from the body and the environment. In animals, the CNS includes the brain and spinal cord.

centriole A cylindrical array of microtubules that is found at the center of a centrosome in animal cells.

centromere A region of a mitotic chromosome that holds sister chromatids together. Microtubules of the spindle fiber connect to an area of the centromere called the kinetochore.

centrosome Organizes the mitotic spindle and the spindle poles. In most animal cells it contains a pair of centrioles.

chiasma (plural: chiasmata) An X-shaped connection between homologous chromosomes that occurs during meiosis I, representing a site of crossing-over, or genetic exchange between the two chromosomes.

chromatid A duplicate chromosome that is still connected to the original at the centromere. The identical pair are called sister chromatids.

chromatin A complex of DNA and proteins (histones and nonhistones) that forms each chromosome and is found in the nucleus of all eukaryotes. Decondensed and threadlike during interphase.

chromatin condensation Compaction of different regions of interphase chromosomes that is mediated by the histones.

chromosome One long molecule of DNA that contains the organism's genes. In prokaryotes, the chromosome is circular and naked; in eukaryotes, it is linear and complexed with histone and nonhistone proteins.

chromosome condensation Compaction of entire chromosomes in preparation for cell division.

clinical breast exam An exam of the breast performed by a physician to check for lumps or other changes.

cyclic adenosine monophosphate (cAMP) A second messenger in a cell-signaling pathway that is produced from ATP by the enzyme adenylate cyclase.

cyclin A protein that activates protein kinases (cyclin-dependent protein kinases, or Cdk) that control progression from one state of the cell cycle to another.

cytochemistry The study of the intracellular distribution of chemicals.

cytochrome Colored, iron-containing protein that is part of the electron transport chain.

cytotoxic T cell A T lymphocyte that kills infected body cells.

dendrite An extension of a nerve cell that receives signals from other neurons.

dexrazoxane A drug used to protect the heart from the toxic effects of anthracycline drugs such as doxorubicin. It belongs to the family of drugs called chemoprotective agents.

dideoxy sequencing A method for sequencing DNA that employs dideoxyribose nucleotides.

diploid A genetic term meaning two sets of homologous chromosomes, one set from the mother and the other from the father. Thus diploid organisms have two versions (alleles) of each gene in the genome.

DNA (deoxyribonucleic acid) A long polymer formed by linking four different kinds of nucleotides together like beads on a string. The sequence of nucleotides is used to encode an organism's genes.

DNA helicase An enzyme that separates and unwinds the two DNA strands in preparation for replication or transcription.

DNA library A collection of DNA fragments that are cloned into plasmids or viral genomes.

DNA ligase An enzyme that joins two DNA strands together to make a continuous DNA molecule.

DNA microarray A technique for studying the simultaneous expression of a very large number of genes.

DNA polymerase An enzyme that synthesizes DNA using one strand as a template.

DNA primase An enzyme that synthesizes a short strand of RNA that serves as a primer for DNA replication.

dorsal The backside of an animal. Also refers to the upper surface of anatomical structures, such as arms or wings.

dorsoventral The body axis running from the backside to the frontside or the upperside to the underside of a structure.

double helix The three-dimensional structure of DNA in which the two strands twist around each other to form a spiral.

doxorubicin An anticancer drug that belongs to a family of antitumor antibiotics.

Drosophila melanogaster Small species of fly, commonly called a fruit fly, that is used as an experimental organism in genetics, embryology, and gerontology.

ductal carcinoma in situ (DCIS) Abnormal cells that involve only the lining of a breast duct. The cells have not spread outside the duct to other tissues in the breast. Also called intraductal carcinoma.

dynein A motor protein that is involved in chromosome movements during cell division.

dysplasia Disordered growth of cells in a tissue or organ, often leading to the development of cancer.

ectoderm An embryonic tissue that is the precursor of the epidermis and the nervous system.

electrochemical gradient A differential concentration of an ion or molecule across the cell membrane that serves as a source of potential energy and may polarize the cell electrically.

electron microscope A microscope that uses electrons to produce a high-resolution image of the cell.

embryogensis The development of an embryo from a fertilized egg.

embryonic stem cell (ES cell) A pluripotent cell derived from the inner cell mass (the cells that give rise to the embryo instead of the placenta) of a mammalian embryo.

endocrine cell A cell that is specialized for the production and release of hormones. Such cells make up hormone-producing tissue such as the pituitary gland or gonads.

endocytosis Cellular uptake of material from the environment by invagination of the cell membrane to form a vesicle called an endosome. The endosome's contents are made available to the cell after it fuses with a lysosome.

endoderm An embryonic tissue layer that gives rise to the gut.

endoplasmic reticulum (ER) Membrane-bounded chambers that are used to modify newly synthesized proteins with the addition of sugar molecules (glycosylation). When finished, the glycosylated proteins are sent to the Golgi apparatus in exocytotic vesicles.

endothelial cell A cell that forms the endothelium, a thin sheet of cells lining the inner surface of all blood vessels.

enhancer A DNA regulatory sequence that provides a binding site for transcription factors capable of increasing the rate of transcription for a specific gene. Often located thousands of base pairs away from the gene it regulates.

enveloped virus A virus containing a capsid that is surrounded by a lipid bilayer originally obtained from the membrane of a previously infected cell.

enzyme A protein or RNA that catalyzes a specific chemical reaction.

epidermis The epithelial layer, or skin, that covers the outer surface of the body.

ER signal sequence The amino terminal sequence that directs proteins to enter the endoplasmic reticulum (ER). This sequence is removed once the protein enters the ER.

erythrocyte A red blood cell that contains the oxygen-carrying pigment hemoglobin used to deliver oxygen to cells in the body.

***Escherichia coli* (*E. coli*)** Rod shape, gram negative bacterium that inhabits the intestinal tract of most animals and is used as an experimental organism by geneticists and biomedical researchers.

euchromatin Lightly staining portion of interphase chromatin, in contrast to the darkly staining heterochromatin (condensed chromatin). Euchromatin contains most, if not all, of the active genes.

eukaryote (eucaryote) A cell containing a nucleus and many membrane-bounded organelles. All life-forms, except bacteria and viruses, are composed of eukaryote cells.

exocytosis The process by which molecules are secreted from a cell. Molecules to be secreted are located in Golgi-derived vesicles that fuse with the inner surface of the cell membrane, depositing the contents into the intercellular space.

exon Coding region of a eukaryote gene that is represented in messenger RNA, and thus directs the synthesis of a specific protein.

expression studies Examination of the type and quantity of mRNA or protein that is produced by cells, tissues, or organs.

fat A lipid material, consisting of triglycerides (fatty acids bound to glycerol), that is stored adipocytes as an energy reserve.

fatty acid A compound that has a carboxylic acid attached to a long hydrocarbon chain. A major source of cellular energy and a component of phospholipids.

filter hybridization The detection of specific DNA or RNA molecules, fixed on a nylon filter, by incubating the filter with a labeled probe that hybridizes to the target sequence.

fertilization The fusion of haploid male and female gametes to form a diploid zygote.

fibroblast The cell type that, by secreting an extracellular matrix, gives rise to the connective tissue of the body.

fixative A chemical that is used to preserve cells and tissues. Common examples are formaldehyde, methanol, and acetic acid.

flagellum (plural: flagella) Whiplike structure found in prokaryotes and eukaryotes that are used to propel cells through water.

fluorescein Fluorescent dye that produces a green light when illuminated with ultraviolet or blue light.

fluorescent dye A dye that absorbs UV or blue light and emits light of a longer wavelength, usually as green or red light.

fluorescent microscope A microscope that is equipped with special filters and a beam splitter for the examination of tissues and cells stained with a fluorescent dye.

follicle cell Cells that surround and help feed a developing oocyte.

G_0 G "zero" refers to a phase of the cell cycle. State of withdrawal from the cycle as the cell enters a resting or quiescent stage. Occurs in differentiated body cells as well as developing oocytes.

G_1 Gap 1 refers to the phase of the cell cycle that occurs just after mitosis and before the next round of DNA synthesis.

G_2 Gap 2 refers to the phase of the cell cycle that follows DNA replication and precedes mitosis.

gap junction A communication channel in the membranes of adjacent cells that allows free passage of ions and small molecules.

gastrulation An embryological event in which a spherical embryo is converted into an elongated structure with a head end, a tail end, and a gut (gastrula).

gene A region of the DNA that specifies a specific protein or RNA molecule that is handed down from one generation to the next. This region includes both the coding, noncoding, and regulatory sequences.

gene regulatory protein Any protein that binds to DNA and thereby affects the expression of a specific gene.

gene repressor protein A protein that binds to DNA and blocks transcription of a specific gene.

gene therapy A method for treating disease whereby a defective gene, causing the disease, is either repaired, replaced, or supplemented with a functional copy.

genetic code A set of rules that assigns a specific DNA or RNA triplet, consisting of a three-base sequence, to a specific amino acid.

genome All of the genes that belong to a cell or an organism.

genomic library A collection of DNA fragments, obtained by digesting genomic DNA with a restriction enzyme, that are cloned into plasmid or viral vectors.

genomics The study of DNA sequences and their role in the function and structure of an organism.

genotype The genetic composition of a cell or organism.

germ cell Cells that develop into gametes, either sperm or oocytes.

glucose Six-carbon monosaccharide (sugar) that is the principal source of energy for many cells and organisms. Stored as glycogen in animal cells and as starch in plants. Wood is an elaborate polymer of glucose and other sugars.

glycerol A three-carbon alcohol that is an important component of phospholipids.

glycocalyx A molecular "forest," consisting of glycosylated proteins and lipids, that covers the surface of every cell. The glycoproteins and glycolipids, carried to the cell membrane by Golgi-derived vesicles, have many functions, including the formation of ion channels, cell-signaling receptors and transporters.

glycogen A polymer of glucose used to store energy in an animal cell.

glycolysis The degradation of glucose with production of ATP.

glycoprotein Any protein that has a chain of glucose molecules (oligosaccharide) attached to some of the amino acid residues.

glycosylation The process of adding one or more sugar molecules to proteins or lipids.

glycosyl transferase An enzyme in the Golgi complex that adds glucose to proteins.

Golgi complex (Golgi apparatus) Membrane-bounded organelle in eukaryote cells that receives glycoproteins from the ER, which are modified and sorted before being sent to their final destination. The Golgi complex is also the source of glycolipids that are destined for the cell membrane. The glycoproteins and glycolipids leave the Golgi by exocytosis. This organelle is named after the Italian histologist Camillo Golgi, who discovered it in 1898.

granulocyte A type of white blood cell that includes the neutrophils, basophils, and eosinophils.

growth factor A small protein (polypeptide) that can stimulate cells to grow and proliferate.

haploid Having only one set of chromosomes. A condition that is typical in gametes, such as sperm and eggs.

HeLa cell A tumor-derived cell line, originally isolated from a cancer patient in 1951. Currently used by many laboratories to study the cell biology of cancer and carcinogenesis.

helix-loop-helix A structural motif common to a group of gene regulatory proteins.

helper T cell A type of T lymphocyte that helps stimulate B cells to make antibodies directed against a specific microbe or antigen.

hemoglobin An iron-containing protein complex, located in red blood cells that picks up oxygen in the lungs and carries it to other tissues and cells of the body.

hemopoiesis Production of blood cells, occurring primarily in the bone marrow.

hepatocyte A liver cell.

heterochromatin A region of a chromosome that is highly condensed and transcriptionally inactive.

histochemistry The study of chemical differentiation of tissues.

histology The study of tissues.

histone Small nuclear proteins, rich in the amino acids arginine and lysine, that form the nucleosome in eukaryote nuclei, a beadlike structure that is a major component of chromatin.

HIV The human immunodeficiency virus that is responsible for AIDS.

homolog One of two or more genes that have a similar sequence and are descended from a common ancestor gene.

homologous Organs or molecules that are similar in structure because they have descended from a common ancestor. Used primarily in reference to DNA and protein sequences.

homologous chromosomes Two copies of the same chromosome, one inherited from the mother and the other from the father.

hormone A signaling molecule, produced and secreted by endocrine glands. Usually released into general circulation for coordination of an animal's physiology.

housekeeping gene A gene that codes for a protein that is needed by all cells, regardless of the cell's specialization. Genes encoding enzymes involved in glycolysis and the Krebs cycle are common examples.

hybridization A term used in molecular biology (recombinant DNA technology) meaning the formation of a double-stranded nucleic acid through complementary base-pairing. A property that is exploited in filter hybridization, a procedure that is used to screen gene libraries and to study gene structure and expression.

hydrophilic A polar compound that mixes readily with water.

hydrophobic A nonpolar molecule that dissolves in fat and lipid solutions but not in water.

hydroxyl group (-OH) Chemical group consisting of oxygen and hydrogen that is a prominent part of alcohol.

image analysis A computerized method for extracting information from digitized microscopic images of cells or cell organelles.

immunofluorescence Detection of a specific cellular protein with the aid of a fluorescent dye that is coupled to an antibody.

immunoglobulin (Ig) An antibody made by B cells as part of the adaptive immune response.

incontinence Inability to control the flow of urine from the bladder (urinary incontinence) or the escape of stool from the rectum (fecal incontinence).

in situ hybridization A method for studying gene expression, whereby a labeled cDNA or RNA probe hybridizes to a specific mRNA in intact cells or tissues. The procedure is usually carried out on tissue sections or smears of individual cells.

insulin Polypeptide hormone secreted by β (beta) cells in the vertebrate pancreas. Production of this hormone is regulated directly by the amount of glucose that is in the blood.

interleukin A small protein hormone, secreted by lymphocytes, to activate and coordinate the adaptive immune response.

interphase The period between each cell division, which includes the G_1, S, and G_2 phases of the cell cycle.

intron A section of a eukaryote gene that is non-coding. It is transcribed, but does not appear in the mature mRNA.

in vitro Refers to cells growing in culture, or a biochemical reaction occurring in a test tube (Latin for "in glass").

in vivo A biochemical reaction, or a process, occurring in living cells or a living organism (Latin for "in life").

ion An atom that has gained or lost electrons, thus acquiring a charge. Common examples are Na^+ and Ca^{++} ions.

ion channel A transmembrane channel that allows ions to diffuse across the membrane and down their electrochemical gradient.

Jak-STAT signaling pathway One of several cell-signaling pathways that activates gene expression. The pathway is activated through cell-surface receptors and cytoplasmic Janus kinases (Jaks), and signal transducers and activators of transcription (STATs).

karyotype A pictorial catalog of a cell's chromosomes, showing their number, size, shape, and overall banding pattern.

keratin Proteins produced by specialized epithelial cells called keratinocytes. Keratin is found in hair, fingernails, and feathers.

kinesin A motor protein that uses energy obtained from the hydrolysis of ATP to move along a microtubule.

kinetochore A complex of proteins that forms around the centromere of mitotic or meiotic chromosomes, providing an attachment site for microtubules. The other end of each microtubule is attached to a chromosome.

Krebs cycle (citric acid cycle) The central metabolic pathway in all eukaryotes and aerobic prokaryotes, discovered by the German chemist Hans Krebs in 1937. The cycle oxidizes acetyl groups derived from food molecules. The end products are CO_2, H_2O, and high-energy electrons, which pass via NADH and FADH2 to the respiratory chain. In eukaryotes, the Krebs cycle is located in the mitochondria.

labeling reaction The addition of a radioactive atom or fluorescent dye to DNA or RNA for use as a probe in filter hybridization.

lagging strand One of the two newly synthesized DNA strands at a replication fork. The lagging strand is synthesized discontinuously, and therefore, its completion lags behind the second, or leading, strand.

lambda bacteriophage A viral parasite that infects bacteria. Widely used as a DNA cloning vector.

leading strand One of the two newly synthesized DNA strands at a replication fork. The leading strand is made by continuous synthesis in the 5' to 3' direction.

leucine zipper A structural motif of DNA binding proteins, in which two identical proteins are joined together at regularly spaced leucine residues, much like a zipper, to form a dimer.

leukemia Cancer of white blood cells.

lipid bilayer Two closely aligned sheets of phospholipids that form the core structure of all cell membranes. The two layers are aligned such that the hydrophobic tails are interior, while the hydrophilic head groups are exterior on both surfaces.

liposome An artificial lipid bilayer vesicle used in membrane studies and as an artificial gene therapy vector.

locus A term from genetics that refers to the position of a gene along a chromosome. Different alleles of the same gene occupy the same locus.

long-term potentiation (LTP) A physical remodeling of synaptic junctions that receive continuous stimulation.

lymphocyte A type of white blood cell that is involved in the adaptive immune response. There are two kinds of lymphocytes: T lymphocytes and B lymphocytes. T lymphocytes (T cells) mature in the thymus and attack invading microbes directly. B lymphocytes (B cells) mature in the bone marrow and make antibodies that are designed to immobilize or destroy specific microbes or antigens.

lysis The rupture of the cell membrane followed by death of the cell.

lysosome Membrane-bounded organelle of eukaryotes that contains powerful digestive enzymes.

macromolecule A very large molecule that is built from smaller molecular subunits. Common examples are DNA, proteins, and polysaccharides.

magnetic resonance imaging (MRI) A procedure in which radio waves and a powerful magnet linked to a computer are used to create detailed pictures of areas inside the body. These pictures can show the difference between normal and diseased tissue. MRI makes better images of organs and soft tissue than other scanning techniques, such as CT or X-ray. MRI is especially useful for imaging the brain, spine, the soft tissue of joints, and the inside of bones. Also called nuclear magnetic resonance imaging.

major histocompatibility complex Vertebrate genes that code for a large family of cell-surface glycoproteins that bind foreign antigens and present them to T cells to induce an immune response.

malignant Refers to the functional status of a cancer cell that grows aggressively and is able to metastasize, or colonize, other areas of the body.

mammography The use of X-rays to create a picture of the breast.

MAP-kinase (mitogen-activated protein kinase) A protein kinase that is part of a cell-proliferation-inducing signaling pathway.

M-cyclin A eukaryote enzyme that regulates mitosis.

meiosis A special form of cell division by which haploid gametes are produced. This is accomplished with two rounds of cell division but only one round of DNA replication.

melanocyte A skin cell that produces the pigment melanin.

membrane The lipid bilayer, and the associated glycocalyx, that surrounds and encloses all cells.

membrane channel A protein complex that forms a pore or channel through the membrane for the free passage of ions and small molecules.

membrane potential A buildup of charged ions on one side of the cell membrane establishes an electrochemical gradient that is measured in millivolts (mV). An important characteristic of neurons as it provides the electric current, when ion channels open, that enable these cells to communicate with each other.

mesoderm An embryonic germ layer that gives rise to muscle, connective tissue, bones, and many internal organs.

messenger RNA (mRNA) An RNA transcribed from a gene that is used as the gene template by the ribosomes, and other components of the translation machinery, to synthesize a protein.

metabolism The sum total of the chemical processes that occur in living cells.

metaphase The stage of mitosis at which the chromosomes are attached to the spindle but have not begun to move apart.

metaphase plate Refers to the imaginary plane established by the chromosomes as they line up at right angles to the spindle poles.

metaplasia A change in the pattern of cellular behavior that often precedes the development of cancer.

metastasis Spread of cancer cells from the site of the original tumor to other parts of the body.

methyl group ($-CH_3$) Hydrophobic chemical group derived from methane. Occurs at the end of a fatty acid.

micrograph Photograph taken through a light, or electron, microscope.

micrometer (μm or micron) Equal to 10^{-6} meters.

microtubule A fine cylindrical tube made of the protein tubulin, forming a major component of the eukaryote cytoskeleton.

millimeter (mm) Equal to 10^{-3} meters.

mitochondrion (plural: mitochondria) Eukaryote organelle, formerly free-living, that produces most of the cell's ATP.

mitogen A hormone or signaling molecule that stimulates cells to grow and divide.

mitosis Division of a eukaryotic nucleus. From the Greek *mitos,* meaning "a thread," in reference to the threadlike appearance of interphase chromosomes.

mitotic chromosome Highly condensed duplicated chromosomes held together by the centromere. Each member of the pair is referred to as a sister chromatid.

mitotic spindle Array of microtubules, fanning out from the polar centrioles and connecting to each of the chromosomes.

molecule Two or more atoms linked together by covalent bonds.

monoclonal antibody An antibody produced from a B cell–derived clonal line. Since all of the cells are clones of the original B cell, the antibodies produced are identical.

monocyte A type of white blood cell that is involved in the immune response.

motif An element of structure or pattern that may be a recurring domain in a variety of proteins.

M phase The period of the cell cycle (mitosis or meiosis) when the chromosomes separate and migrate to the opposite poles of the spindle.

multipass transmembrane protein A membrane protein that passes back and forth across the lipid bilayer.

mutant A genetic variation within a population.

mutation A heritable change in the nucleotide sequence of a chromosome.

myelin sheath Insulation applied to the axons of neurons. The sheath is produced by oligodendrocytes in the central nervous system and by Schwann cells in the peripheral nervous system.

myeloid cell White blood cells other than lymphocytes.

myoblast Muscle precursor cell. Many myoblasts fuse into a syncytium, containing many nuclei, to form a single muscle cell.

myocyte A muscle cell.

NAD (nicotine adenine dinucleotide) Accepts a hydride ion (H^-), produced by the Krebs cycle, forming NADH, the main carrier of electrons for oxidative phosphorylation.

NADH dehydrogenase Removes electrons from NADH and passes them down the electron transport chain.

nanometer (nm) Equal to 10^{-9} meters or 10^{-3} microns.

natural killer cell (NK cell) A lymphocyte that kills virus-infected cells in the body. It also kills foreign cells associated with a tissue or organ transplant.

neuromuscular junction A special form of synapse between a motor neuron and a skeletal muscle cell.

neuron A cell specially adapted for communication that forms the nervous system of all animals.

neurotransmitter A chemical released by neurons at a synapse that transmits a signal to another neuron.

non-small-cell lung cancer A group of lung cancers that includes squamous cell carcinoma, adenocarcinoma, and large cell carcinoma. The small cells are endocrine cells.

northern blotting A technique for the study of gene expression. Messenger RNA (mRNA) is fractionated on an agarose gel and then transferred to a piece of nylon filter paper (or membrane). A specific mRNA is detected by hybridization with a labeled DNA or RNA probe. The original blotting technique invented by E. M. Southern inspired the name.

nuclear envelope The double membrane (two lipid bilayers) enclosing the cell nucleus.

nuclear localization signal (NLS) A short amino acid sequence located on proteins that are destined for the cell nucleus after they are translated in the cytoplasm.

nucleic acid DNA or RNA, a macromolecule consisting of a chain of nucleotides.

nucleolar organizer Region of a chromosome containing a cluster of ribosomal RNA genes that gives rise to the nucleolus.

nucleolus A structure in the nucleus where ribosomal RNA is transcribed and ribosomal subunits are assembled.

nucleoside A purine or pyrimidine linked to a ribose or deoxyribose sugar.

nucleosome A beadlike structure, consisting of histone proteins.

nucleotide A nucleoside containing one or more phosphate groups linked to the 5' carbon of the ribose sugar. DNA and RNA are nucleotide polymers.

nucleus Eukaryote cell organelle that contains the DNA genome on one or more chromosomes.

oligodendrocyte A myelinating glia cell of the vertebrate central nervous system.

oligo labeling A method for incorporating labeled nucleotides into a short piece of DNA or RNA. Also known as the random-primer labeling method.

oligomer A short polymer, usually consisting of amino acids (oligopeptides), sugars (oligosaccharides), or nucleotides (oligonucleotides). Taken from the Greek word *oligos,* meaning "few" or "little."

oncogene A mutant form of a normal cellular gene, known as a proto-oncogene, that can transform a cell to a cancerous phenotype.

oocyte A female gamete or egg cell.

operator A region of a prokaryote chromosome that controls the expression of adjacent genes.

operon Two or more prokaryote genes that are transcribed into a single mRNA.

organelle A membrane-bounded structure, occurring in eukaryote cells, that has a specialized function. Examples are the nucleus, Golgi complex, and endoplasmic reticulum.

osmosis The movement of solvent across a semipermeable membrane that separates a solution with a high concentration of solutes from one with a low concentration of solutes. The membrane must be permeable to the solvent but not to the solutes. In the context of cellular osmosis, the solvent is always water, the solutes are ions and molecules, and the membrane is the cell membrane.

osteoblast Cells that form bones.

ovulation Rupture of a mature follicle with subsequent release of a mature oocyte from the ovary.

oxidative phosphorylation Generation of high-energy electrons from food molecules that are used to power the synthesis of ATP from ADP and inorganic phosphate. The electrons are eventually transferred to oxygen to complete the process. Occurs in bacteria and mitochondria.

p53 A tumor-suppressor gene that is mutated in about half of all human cancers. The normal function of the *p53* protein is to block passage through the cell cycle when DNA damage is detected.

parthenogenesis A natural form of animal cloning whereby an individual is produced without the formation of haploid gametes and the fertilization of an egg.

pathogen An organism that causes disease.

PCR (polymerase chain reaction) A method for amplifying specific regions of DNA by temperature cycling a reaction mixture containing the template, a heat-stable DNA polymerase, and replication primers.

peptide bond The chemical bond that links amino acids together to form a protein.

pH Measures the acidity of a solution as a negative logarithmic function (p) of H^+ concentration (H). Thus a pH of 2.0 (10^{-2} molar H^+) is acidic, whereas a pH of 8.0 (10^{-8} molar H^+) is basic.

phagocyte A cell that engulfs other cells or debris by phagocytosis.

phagocytosis A process whereby cells engulf other cells or organic material by endocytosis. A common practice among protozoans and cells of the vertebrate immune system. (Derived from the Greek word *phagein,* "to eat.")

phenotype Physical characteristics of a cell or organism.

phospholipid The kind of lipid molecule used to construct cell membranes. Composed of a hydrophilic head-group, phosphate, glycerol, and two hydrophobic fatty acid tails.

phosphorylation A chemical reaction in which a phosphate is covalently bonded to another molecule.

photoreceptor A molecule or cell that responds to light.

photosynthesis A biochemical process in which plants, algae, and certain bacteria use energy obtained from sunlight to synthesize macromolecules from CO_2 and H_2O.

phylogeny The evolutionary history of an organism, or group of organisms, often represented diagrammatically as a phylogenetic tree.

pinocytosis A form of endocytosis whereby fluid is brought into the cell from the environment.

placebo An inactive substance that looks the same, and is administered in the same way, as a drug in a clinical trial.

plasmid A minichromosome, often carrying antibiotic-resistant genes, that occurs naturally among prokaryotes. Used extensively as a DNA cloning vector.

platelet A cell fragment, derived from megakaryocytes and lacking a nucleus, that is present in the bloodstream and is involved in blood coagulation.

ploidy The total number of chromosomes (n) that a cell has. Ploidy is also measured as the amount of DNA (C) in a given cell relative to a haploid nucleus of the same organism. Most organisms are diploid, having two sets of chromosomes, one from each parent, but there is great variation among plants and animals. The silk gland of the moth *Bombyx mori,* for example, has cells that are extremely polyploid, reaching values of 100,000C. Flowers are often highly polyploid, and vertebrate hepatocytes may be 16C.

point mutation A change in DNA, particularly in a region containing a gene, that alters a single nucleotide.

polyploid Possessing more than two sets of homologous chromosomes.

portal system A system of liver vessels that carries liver enzymes directly to the digestive tract.

probe Usually a fragment of a cloned DNA molecule that is labeled with a radioisotope or fluorescent dye and used to detect specific DNA or RNA molecules on Southern or northern blots.

promoter A DNA sequence to which RNA polymerase binds to initiate gene transcription.

prophase The first stage of mitosis. The chromosomes are duplicated and beginning to condense but are attached to the spindle.

protein A major constituent of cells and organisms. Proteins, made by linking amino acids together, are used for structural purposes and regulate many biochemical reactions in their alternative role as enzymes. Proteins range in size from just a few amino acids to more than 200.

protein glycosylation The addition of sugar molecules to a protein.

proto-oncogene A normal gene that can be converted to a cancer-causing gene (oncogene) by a point mutation or through inappropriate expression.

protozoa Free-living, single-cell eukaryotes that feed on bacteria and other microorganisms. Common examples are *Paramecium* and *Amoeba.* Parasitic forms are also known that inhabit the digestive and urogenital tract of many animals, including humans.

purine A nitrogen-containing compound that is found in RNA and DNA. Two examples are adenine and guanine.

pyrimidine A nitrogen-containing compound found in RNA and DNA. Examples are cytosine, thymine, and uracil (RNA only).

radioactive isotope An atom with an unstable nucleus that emits radiation as it decays.

randomized clinical trial A study in which the participants are assigned by chance to separate groups that compare different treatments; neither the researchers nor the participants can choose which group. Using chance to assign people to groups means that the groups will be similar and that the treatments they receive can be compared objectively. At the time of the trial, it is not known which treatment is best.

reagent A chemical solution designed for a specific biochemical or histochemical procedure.

recombinant DNA A DNA molecule that has been formed by joining two or more fragments from different sources.

regulatory sequence A DNA sequence to which proteins bind that regulate the assembly of the transcriptional machinery.

replication bubble Local dissociation of the DNA double helix in preparation for replication. Each bubble contains two replication forks.

replication fork The Y-shaped region of a replicating chromosome. Associated with replication bubbles.

replication origin (origin of replication, ORI) The location at which DNA replication begins.

respiratory chain (electron transport chain) A collection of iron- and copper-containing proteins, located in the inner mitochondrion membrane, that utilize the energy of electrons traveling down the chain to synthesize ATP.

restriction enzyme An enzyme that cuts DNA at specific sites.

restriction map The size and number of DNA fragments obtained after digesting with one or more restriction enzymes.

retrovirus A virus that converts its RNA genome to DNA once it has infected a cell.

reverse transcriptase An RNA-dependent DNA polymerase. This enzyme synthesizes DNA by using RNA as a template, the reverse of the usual flow of genetic information from DNA to RNA.

ribosomal RNA (rRNA) RNA that is part of the ribosome and serves both a structural and functional role, possibly by catalyzing some of the steps involved in protein synthesis.

ribosome A complex of protein and RNA that catalyzes the synthesis of proteins.

rough endoplasmic reticulum (rough ER) Endoplasmic reticulum that has ribosomes bound to its outer surface.

Saccharomyces Genus of budding yeast that are frequently used in the study of eukaryote cell biology.

sarcoma Cancer of connective tissue.

Schwann cell Glia cell that produces myelin in the peripheral nervous system.

screening Checking for disease when there are no symptoms.

senescence Physical and biochemical changes that occur in cells and organisms with age.

signal transduction A process by which a signal is relayed to the interior of a cell where it elicits a response at the cytoplasmic or nuclear level.

smooth muscle cell Muscles lining the intestinal tract and arteries. Lacks the striations typical of cardiac and skeletal muscle, giving it a smooth appearance when viewed under a microscope.

somatic cell Any cell in a plant or animal except those that produce gametes (germ cells or germ cell precursors).

somatic cell nuclear transfer Animal cloning technique whereby a somatic cell nucleus is transferred to an enucleated oocyte. Synonomous with cell nuclear replacement.

Southern blotting The transfer of DNA fragments from an agarose gel to a piece of nylon filter paper. Specific fragments are identified by hybridizing the filter to a labeled probe. Invented by the Scottish scientist E. M. Southern in 1975.

stem cell Pluripotent progenitor cell, found in embryos and various parts of the body, that can differentiate into a wide variety of cell types.

steroid A hydrophobic molecule with a characteristic four-ringed structure. Sex hormones, such as estrogen and testosterone, are steroids.

structural gene A gene that codes for a protein or an RNA. Distinguished from regions of the DNA that are involved in regulating gene expression but are non-coding.

synapse A neural communication junction between an axon and a dendrite. Signal transmission occurs when neurotransmitters, released into the junction by the axon of one neuron, stimulate receptors on the dendrite of a second neuron.

syncytium A large multinucleated cell. Skeletal muscle cells are syncytiums produced by the fusion of many myoblasts.

syngeneic transplants A patient receives tissue or an organ from an identical twin.

tamoxifen A drug that is used to treat breast cancer. Tamoxifen blocks the effects of the hormone estrogen in the body. It belongs to the family of drugs called antiestrogens.

T cell (T lymphocyte) A white blood cell involved in activating and coordinating the immune response.

telomere The end of a chromosome. Replaced by the enzyme telomerase with each round of cell division to prevent shortening of the chromosomes.

telophase The final stage of mitosis in which the chromosomes decondense and the nuclear envelope reforms.

template A single strand of DNA or RNA whose sequence serves as a guide for the synthesis of a complementary, or daughter, strand.

therapeutic cloning The cloning of a human embryo for the purpose of harvesting the inner cell mass (ES cells).

topoisomerase An enzyme that makes reversible cuts in DNA to relieve strain or to undo knots.

transcription The copying of a DNA sequence into RNA, catalyzed by RNA polymerase.

transcriptional factor A general term referring to a wide assortment of proteins needed to initiate or regulate transcription.

transfection Introduction of a foreign gene into a eukaryote cell.

transfer RNA (tRNA) A collection of small RNA molecules that transfer an amino acid to a growing polypeptide chain on a ribosome. There is a separate tRNA for amino acid.

transgenic organism A plant or animal that has been transfected with a foreign gene.

trans-Golgi network The membrane surfaces where glycoproteins and glycolipids exit the Golgi complex in transport vesicles.

translation A ribosome-catalyzed process whereby the nucleotide sequence of a mRNA is used as a template to direct the synthesis of a protein.

transposable element (transposon) A segment of DNA that can move from one region of a genome to another.

ultrasound (ultrasonography) A procedure in which high-energy sound waves (ultrasound) are bounced off internal tissues or organs producing echoes that are used to form a picture of body tissues (a sonogram).

umbilical cord blood stem cells Stem cells, produced by a human fetus and the placenta, that are found in the blood that passes from the placenta to the fetus.

vector A virus or plasmid used to carry a DNA fragment into a bacterial cell (for cloning) or into a eukaryote to produce a transgenic organism.

vesicle A membrane-bounded bubble found in eukaryote cells. Vesicles carry material from the ER to the Golgi and from the Golgi to the cell membrane.

virus A particle containing an RNA or DNA genome surrounded by a protein coat. Viruses are cellular parasites that cause many diseases.

western blotting The transfer of protein from a polyacrylamide gel to a piece of nylon filter paper. Specific proteins are detected with labeled antibodies. The name was inspired by the original blotting technique invented by E. M. Southern.

yeast Common term for unicellular eukaryotes that are used to brew beer and make bread. Bakers yeast, *Saccharomyces cerevisiae,* is also widely used in studies on cell biology.

zygote A diploid cell produced by the fusion of a sperm and egg.

FURTHER READING

Alberts, Bruce. *Essential Cell Biology.* New York: Garland Publishing, 1998.

American Institute for Cancer Research. "Diets High in Fiber Cut Risk of Colon Cancer Nearly in Half." May 2, 2003. Available online. URL: http://www.aicr.org/presscorner/pubsearchdetail.lasso?index=1619. Accessed October 23, 2003.

———. "New Scientific Thinking Implicates Body Fat as Cancer Promoter." July 11, 2002. Available online. URL: http://www.aicr.org. Accessed October 23, 2003.

———. "New Theory May Provide Missing Link between Overweight, Cancer." November 16, 2001. Available online. URL: http://www.aicr.org/action.lasso?-Database=w005aicr.fp3&-Layout=WEB&-Response=pubsearchdetail.htm&-RecordID=32929. Accessed October 23, 2003.

Associated Press. "WHO: Tobacco Even More Cancerous." Available online. URL: http://apnews.excite.com/article/20020619/D7K8DSC01.html. Accessed October 23, 2003.

BioMedNet. "Early Success for Cancer Genome Project." May 26, 2002. Available online. URL: http://news.bmn.com/conferences/list/view?fileyear=2002&fileacronyn=ESHG&fi leday=day2&pagefile=story_4.html. Accessed October 23, 2003.

ClinicalTrials.gov. "Gene Therapy Clinical Trials." Available online. URL: http://clinicaltrials.gov/search/term=gene%2Btherapy. Accessed October 23, 2003.

Genetics and Public Policy Center. "The Regulatory Environment for Human Gene Therapy." April 2003. Available online. URL: http://www.dnapolicy.org/policy/humanGeneTransfer.jhtml. Accessed October 23, 2003.

Genetic Science Learning Center, University of Utah. "Human Genetics." Available online. URL: http://gslc.genetics.utah.edu. Accessed October 23, 2003.

IMB Jena (Institute for Molecular Biotechnology). "Molecules of Life." Available online. URL: http://www.imb-jena.de/IMAGE.html. Accessed October 23, 2003.

Krstic, R. V. *Illustrated Encyclopedia of Human Histology.* New York: Springer-Verlag, 1984.

Lentz, Thomas L. *Cell Fine Structure: An Atlas of Drawings of Whole-Cell Structure.* Philadelphia: Saunders, 1971.

Mader, Sylvia S. *Inquiry into Life.* Boston: McGraw-Hill, 2003.

National Cancer Institute. "Newly Approved Cancer Treatments." Available online. URL: http://www.cancer.gov/templates/pageprint.aspx?viewid=18bb4bd0-735f-4046-92fc-4663a7aca419. Accessed October 23, 2003.

National Center for Biotechnology Information. "Genes and Disease." Chromosome maps of all genes known to cause human diseases. Available online. URL: http://www.ncbi.nlm.nih.gov/books/bv.fcgi?call=bv.View..ShowSection&rid=gnd.preface.9. Accessed October 23, 2003.

National Institutes of Health. "Stem Cell Information." Available online. URL: http://stemcells.nih.gov/index.asp. Accessed October 23, 2003.

———. "Stem Cells: A Primer." May 2000. Available online. URL: http://www.nih.gov/news/stemcell/primer.html. Accessed October 23, 2003.

National Toxicology Program. "National Toxicology Program Report on Carcinogens." Available online. URL: http://ntp-server.niehs.nih.gov/NewHomeRoc/AboutRoC.html. Accessed October 23, 2003.

Nature. "Double Helix: 50 Years of DNA." Many articles were assembled by the journal to commemorate the 50th anniversary of James Watson and Francis Crick's classic paper describing the structure of DNA. Available online. URL: http://www.nature.com/nature/dna50/index.html. Accessed October 23, 2003.

———. "A Subway Map of Cancer Pathways." Available online. URL: http://www.nature.com/nrc/journal/v2/n5/weinbergposter/index.html. Accessed October 23, 2003.

Nature Reviews, 2003. "Apoptosis: Cheating Death." Available online. URL: http://www.nature.com/cgi-af/DynaPage.taf?file=/nrc/journal/v3/n2/full/nrc1009_fs.html. Accessed October 23, 2003.

———. "Carcinogenesis: Double Whammy." Available online. URL: http://www.nature.com/cgi-af/DynaPage.taf?file=/nrc/journal/v3/n2/full/nrc1000_fs.html. Accessed October 23, 2003.

———. "Curing Metastatic Cancer: Lessons from Testicular Germ-Cell Tumours." Available online. URL: http://www.nature.com/cgi-taf/DynaPage.taf?file=/nrc/journal/v3/n7/abs/nrc1120_fs.html. Accessed October 23, 2003.

———. "Radiotherapy: Two-pronged Attack." Available online. URL: http://www.nature.com/cgi-taf/DynaPage.taf?file=/nrc/journal/v3/n7/full/nrc1129_fs.html. Accessed October 23, 2003.

———. "Tumour Suppressors: A Greater Loss." Available online. URL: http://www.nature.com/cgi-taf/DynaPage.taf?file=/nrc/journal/v3/n2/full/nrc1005_fs.html. Accessed October 23, 2003.

———. "Umbilical-Cord Blood Transplantation for the Treatment of Cancer." Available online. URL: http://www.nature.com/cgi-taf/DynaPage.taf?file=/nrc/journal/v3/n7/abs/nrc1125_fs.html. Accessed October 23, 2003.

New York Times. "Bone Marrow Found to Have Cells to Repair the Pancreas." March 15, 2003. Available online. URL: http://www.nytimes.com/2003/03/15/health/15STEM.html. Accessed October 23, 2003.

———. "Cancer Pioneer Aims to Market a Vaccine." August 19, 2003. Available online. URL: http://www.nytimes.com/2003/08/19/science/19PROF.html. Accessed October 23, 2003.

———. "Politically Correct Stem Cell Is Licensed to Biotech Concern." December 11, 2002. Available online. URL: http://www.nytimes.com/2002/12/11/business/11STEM.html. Accessed October 23, 2003.

———. "Scientist Quits after Claims He Faked Data." June 14, 2003. Available online. URL: http://www.nytimes.com/2003/06/14/health/14CANC.html. Accessed October 23, 2003.

———. "U.S. Study Hails Stem Cells' Promise." June 27, 2001. Available online. URL: http://www.nytimes.com/2001/06/27/politics/27RESE.html. Accessed October 23, 2003.

Oak Ridge National Laboratory. "Gene Therapy." Available online. URL: http://www.ornl.gov/TechResources/Human_Genome/medicine/genetherapy.html. Accessed October 23, 2003.

Scientific American. "Bone Marrow Stem Cells Reach Brain and Acclimate." January 22, 2003. Available online. URL: http://www.scientificamerican.com/article.cfm?chanID=sa003&articleID=0009B400B9F5-1E2D-8B3B809EC588EEDF. Accessed October 23, 2003.

———. "Cell Communication: The Inside Story." June 20, 2000. Available online. URL: http://www.sciam.com/printversion.cfm?articleID=0001998E-5F5A1C74-9B81809EC588EF21. Accessed October 23, 2003.

———. "Changing Cancer Cells' Surface Sugars Can Inhibit Tumor Growth." January 22, 2002. Available online. URL: http://www.sciam.com/print_version.cfm?articleID=0000BE67-BF37-1CCEB4A8809EC588 EEDF. Accessed October 23, 2003.

———. "A New Skin Cancer Culprit." February 26, 2001. Available online. URL: http://www.sciam.com/print_version.cfm?articleID=0006A278-DC54-1C5AB882809EC588ED9F. Accessed October 23, 2003.

———. "Tumor Cells Leave Chemicals in Their Wake to Help Cancer Spread." September 4, 2001. Available online. URL: http://www.sciam.com/print_version.cfm?articleID=00076454-5C0C-1C61B882809EC588ED9F. Accessed October 23, 2003.

University of Leicester. "Virus Families." Available online. URL: http://www.micro.msb.le.ac.uk/3035/3035virusfamilies.html. Accessed October 23, 2003.

U.S. Food and Drug Administration. "Cellular and Gene Therapy." Available online. URL: http://www.fda.gov/cber/gene.html. Accessed October 23, 2003.

WEB SITES

Center for Biologics Evaluation and Research. FDA center responsible for monitoring gene therapy. http://www.fda.gov/cber/about. html. Accessed October 23, 2003.

The Department of Energy Human Genome Project (United States). Covers every aspect of the human genome project, including applications to gene therapy. http://www.ornl.gov/TechResources/ Human_ Genome. Accessed October 23, 2003.

Gene Therapy Advisory Committee (United Kingdom). http:// www.doh.gov.uk/genetics/gtac/index.html. Accessed October 23, 2003.

Gene Therapy Department, University of Southern California. http://www.humangenetherapy.com. Accessed October 23, 2003.

Genetic Science Learning Center at the Eccles Institute of Human Genetics, University of Utah. An excellent resource for beginning students. This site contains information and illustrations covering basic cell biology, animal cloning, gene therapy, and stem cells. http://gslc.genetics.utah.edu. Accessed October 23, 2003.

Institute of Molecular Biotechnology, Jena/Germany. Image Library of Biological Macromolecules. http://www.imb-jena.de/IMAGE. html. Accessed October 23, 2003.

International Agency for Research on Cancer. http://www.iarc.fr. Accessed October 23, 2003.

The Journal of Gene Medicine. Provides links to gene therapy trials. http://www.wiley.co.uk/genetherapy/clinical. Accessed October 23, 2003.

National Center for Biotechnology Information (NCBI). This site, established by the National Institutes of Health, is an excellent resource for anyone interested in biology. The NCBI provides access to GenBank (DNA sequences), literature databases (Medline and others), molecular databases, and topics dealing with genomic biology. With the literature database, for example, anyone can access Medline's 11,000,000 biomedical journal citations to research biomedical questions. Many of these links provide free access to full-text research papers. http://www.ncbi. nlm.nih.gov. Accessed October 23, 2003.

The National Human Genome Research Institute (United States). The institute supports genetic and genomic research, including the ethical, legal, and social implications of genetics research. http://www. genome.gov. Accessed October 23, 2003.

National Institute of Health (United States). Links to cancer articles and statistics. http://www.ncbi.nlm.nih.gov. Accessed October 23, 2003.

National Toxicology Program. Established by the National Institutes of Health, this site provides detailed information about carcinogens. http://ntp-server.niehs.nih.gov. Accessed October 23, 2003.

Nature. The journal *Nature* has provided a comprehensive guide to the human genome. This site provides links to the definitive historical record for the sequences and analyses of human chromosomes. All papers, which are free for downloading, are based on the final draft produced by the Human Genome Project. http://www.nature.com/nature/focus/humangenome. Accessed October 23, 2003.

The Sanger Institute (United Kingdom). DNA sequencing center, named after Fred Sanger, inventor of the most commonly used method for sequencing DNA. The institute is also involved in projects that apply human DNA sequence data to find cures for cancer and other medical disorders. http://www.sanger.ac.uk. Accessed October 9, 2003.

The World Health Organization. Extensive coverage of cancer rates and types throughout the world. http://www.who.int/en. Accessed October 23, 2003.

INDEX

Italic page numbers indicate illustrations.

A

A antigen 111–113, *114*
ABO blood group system 111–113, *114*
accelerators, linear 53
actin filaments *77,* 78
actinic keratosis 18
adenine 80
adenocarcinomas 3
adenomas 2–3, 72
adenosine deaminase deficiency 110
adenosine diphosphate (ADP) 80, 94
adenosine monophosphate (AMP) 80, 94
adenosine triphosphate (ATP)
  production of 78, 94
  structure of 80
adenoviruses *108,* 109
adipocytes 60–61
ADP. *See* adenosine diphosphate
Adriamycin. *See* doxorubicin
Aflatoxin 39
Africa, incidence of cancer in 55–57, *56,* 59
African Americans, prostate cancer among 15
agarose gel *97,* 102, 103–104, *106*
age
  and bladder cancer 4
  and brain tumors 6
  incidence and 37–38
  and leukemia 11
  and multiple genetic mutations 25
  and prostate cancer 15
AIDS virus *108,* 109
alcohol consumption 62
allogeneic bone marrow transplants 46
American Society of Clinical Oncology (ASCO) 69
amino acids
  genetic coding for 92–94, *93*
  peptide bonds between 80
  structure of 78, *79*
  types of 78
AMP. *See* adenosine monophosphate
anaphase
  of meiosis I 88
  of mitosis 85–87, *86*
anemia
  bone marrow stimulants and 45
  from chemotherapy 49
  sickle-cell 107–109
angiogenesis
  definition of 24, 42
  during development 42–43
  functions of 42–43
  in metastasis 24, 43
  regulation of 43
  targeted in therapy 43
angiogenesis blockers 42–43
animal cloning viii
animal experimentation 67, 68
antibodies, monoclonal 45
antigens
  A and B 111–113
  cell-surface 46, 111–115
  human leukocyte 113–114
  in tissue matching 111–115
apoptosis
  definition of 24
  after detection of errors, in normal cells 24, 25–26, 28
  lack of, in cancer cells 24
  p53 gene in 31
  T cell regulation of 30
Archaea 76
areola 8
argon laser 52
asbestos 39
  as carcinogen 39, 65
  and lung cancer 14, 39
ASCO. *See* American Society of Clinical Oncology

Asia, incidence of cancer in 55–57, *56*
Aspergillus oryzae 39
aspirin, and colon cancer 72
astrocytes 6
astrocytomas 6
ATP. *See* adenosine triphosphate
ATP synthetase 94
autogeneic bone marrow transplants 46
autoimmunity 73–74

B

BACs. *See* bacterial artificial chromosomes
bacteria
  evolution of 76
  human genes obtained from 117
  plasmids of 98
bacterial artificial chromosomes (BACs) 116
bacteriophage 100
bacteriophage G4 genome 115
B antigen 111–113, *114*
basal cell carcinoma 3, 16–18
basal cells 16, *17*
B cells. *See* B lymphocytes
benign tumors
  definition of 2
  switch from malignant to 36
benzopyrene 40, 41
beta-napthylamine 39
bevacizumab 43
bicalutamide 48
biopsy
  in breast cancer diagnosis 9
  in leukemia diagnosis 11
biotechnology, rise of vii–viii
biotherapies 44–45
Bishop, J. Michael 34
bladder, anatomy of 4
bladder cancer 4–5
  beta-napthylamine and 39
  diagnosis of 5
  incidence of
    by continent *56*
    in developed *vs.* undeveloped countries *58, 60*
  mortality rates for 4
  risk factors for 4
  stages of 5
  symptoms of 5
blood cells
  anatomy of 10–11
  types of 10–11
blood clotting, chemotherapy and 49
blood-forming tissues, cancers of. *See* leukemia
blood group system, ABO 111–113, *114*
blood vessels, formation of. *See* angiogenesis
blotting, Southern and northern 103–104, *106*
B lymphocytes (B cells)
  in biotherapy 44
  functions of 44
  monoclonal antibodies produced by 45
bone marrow
  in leukemia diagnosis 11
  stem cell therapy for 54
bone marrow stimulants 44–45
bone marrow transplantation 46
  vs. stem cell therapy 54
  types of 46
brain, anatomy of 5–6, *6*
brain stem 5, 6
brain tumors 5–8
  diagnosis of *7*, 8
  incidence of
    by continent *56*
    in developed *vs.* undeveloped countries *58, 60*
  mortality rates for 2
  rarity of 5
  risk factors for 6
  as secondary tumors 6
  stages of 8
  symptoms of 7–8
BRCA1 gene, and breast cancer 9
BRCA2 gene, and breast cancer 9
breast, anatomy of 8
breast cancer 8–10
  clinical trials on 69–71
  diagnosis of 9
  diet and 62
  estrogen and 9, 47–48
  incidence of
    by continent *56*
    in developed *vs.* undeveloped countries *58, 60*
  risk factors for 9
  stages of 9–10
  symptoms of 9
  types of 8–9

C

cadherins 36
Caenorhabditis elegans 116
cancer(s). *See also* specific types
  common types of 1–18
  discovery of cause of xi–xii
  naming conventions for 2–3
cancer cells 19–26
  broken chromosomes and 21–22
  communication failure with 23–24

damage checkpoints in 30
evolution of 25–26, 27–28
freedom of movement for 24–25, 36
immortality of 19–21
irregular surface of *20*
malignant 36
multiple genetic mutations in 25–26
single, tumors formed from 35
transformation into 2
Cancer Research Network 70–71
carbon dioxide laser 52
carcinogens 38–41
definition of 38
environmental 39, 65
NIH list of 38–39
in tobacco products 14, 39–41
carcinomas *10*. *See also* specific types
definition of 2
lung cancer as 13
catheters 48
CBE. *See* clinical breast exam
CDC. *See* Centers for Disease Control
cDNA. *See* complimentary DNA
cell(s) 76–95. *See also* specific types
in biotechnology vii–viii
cancer (*See* cancer cells)
cycle of 28–30, *29*, *84*, 84–85
damage checkpoints in *29*, 29–30
division of (*See* meiosis; mitosis)
macromolecules of 80–84, *81*
molecules of 78–80, *79*
organelles of 76–78, *77*
suicide of (*See* apoptosis)
cell phone radiation, brain tumors and 6
cell-surface antigens 46, 111–115
Centers for Disease Control (CDC) 59
central nervous system (CNS) 5–6, *6*
centromere 85, *86*
centrosome *77*, 78
cerebellum 5, 6
cerebrum 5, 6
chemical carcinogens 39
chemotherapy 47–49
administration of 48
clinical trials on 71–72
mechanism of 47–48
side effects of 48–49
types of 48–49
CHF. *See* congestive heart failure
chickens, sarcomas in xi, xii, 33
childbearing, late, and breast cancer 9
children, leukemia in 11
China, prostate cancer in 59
chondromas 3
chondrosarcomas 3
chromosomes
broken/abnormal, and cancer cells 21–22
in meiosis 87–90, *89*
in mitosis 85–87, *86*
Philadelphia *21*, 22, 35
segregation of, regulation of 26
telomeres on 20–21
cigarette smoking. *See* tobacco use
cigar smoking. *See* tobacco use
cisplatin 47
clinical breast exam (CBE) 9, 69–70
clinical trials 67–75
application procedure for 67–68
on breast cancer 69–71
on chemotherapy 71–72
on colon cancer 72
on gene therapy 50–51, 110–111
on lung cancer 72–73
on melanoma 73–74
on metastasis 74–75
phases of 67–69
cloning viii, 98–100, 101
cloning vector 109
CNS. *See* central nervous system
cobalt-60 53
codons 92, *93*
cold, common 107, 109
colon cancer
clinical trials on 72
diet and 62
incidence of
by continent *56*
in developed *vs.* undeveloped countries *58*, *60*
colony-stimulating factor (CSF) 45, 49
colorectal adenomas 72
communication, cellular, and cancer cells 23–24
complimentary DNA (cDNA) 100–101, 105
complimentary DNA (cDNA) libraries 100–101
computed tomography (CT) scans, of brain tumors 8
computer-based radiotherapy 53
congestive heart failure (CHF), doxorubicin and 71–72

connective tissue, cancers of. *See* sarcomas
consent, informed, for clinical trials 68
contact inhibition, in cells 23–24
contigs 116
coronaviruses 109
cryoprobe 50
cryosurgery 50
CSF. *See* colony-stimulating factor
CT. *See* computed tomography
CTLA-4. *See* cytotoxic T lymphocyte-associated antigen 4
cytochrome b 94
cytochrome oxidase 94
cytokines
  in biotherapy 44
  T cell secretion of 44
cytokinesis 87
cytosine 80
cytoskeleton *77,* 78
cytotoxic T lymphocyte-associated antigen 4 (CTLA-4) 73–74

D

dATP. *See* deoxyadenine triphosphate
daughter cells, production of
  damage checkpoints in 30
  in meiosis 88, *89,* 90
  in mitosis 87
  regulation of 26
dCTP. *See* deoxycytosine triphosphate
deoxyadenine triphosphate (dATP) 101
deoxycytosine triphosphate (dCTP) 101
deoxyribonucleotides 101
deoxyribose 80
Department of Energy (DOE), and human genome project 115
dermis, anatomy of 16
DeSilva, Ashi 110
developed countries, cancer rates in 57–59, *58*
  diet and 59–62
dexrazoxane 71–72
dideoxynucleotides 102
diet
  North American 59–62, 66
  and prostate cancer 15, 61
digital rectal exam (DRE) 15
disaccharides 83–84
diseases, infectious 107
DNA 96–107
  chemotherapy drugs targeting 47
  cloning of viii, 98–100, 101
  damage checkpoints for 30
  enzymes modifying 96–98
  fluorescent in situ hybridization of 105
  functions of 82
  libraries of 100–101
  nucleotides in 80, 92
  polymerase chain reaction in 107
  sequencing of 101–103, *102, 103, 105,* 115–117
  Southern and northern blotting of 103–104
  structure of *81,* 82, *83*
  transcription and translation of 92, 117
DNA adducts *40,* 40–41
DNA helicase 90, *91*
DNA ligase 96, 98, 109
DNA polymerase 90, *91,* 101, 102, 107
DNA replication 90, *91*
  and DNA sequencing 101–103
  and labeling cloned DNA 101
  telomeres in 20–21
DNA synthesis (S phase) 84, 90
  chemotherapy drugs blocking 47
  damage checkpoints in 29–30
docetaxel 73
DOE. *See* Department of Energy
dosage, in phase I clinical trials 68
double helix 82
doxorubicin 47
  clinical studies on 71–72
DRE. *See* digital rectal exam
Drosophila 116
drugs, cancer. *See* chemotherapy; specific drugs
ductal carcinoma 8–9
ducts, breast 8–9
Dutch MRI Screening Study 69–70

E

*Eco*RI 98
edema, with brain tumors 7
effectiveness, of breast cancer screening methods 69–70
electron transport chain 78, 94
endoplasmic reticulum (ER) 76–78, *77*
endostatin 43
environment, carcinogens in 65

enzymes. *See also* specific enzymes
DNA-modifying 96–98
role in genes 30
epidermis, anatomy of 16, *17*
epithelial cells
cancers of (*See* carcinomas)
susceptibility to cancer 1
ER. *See* endoplasmic reticulum
erythrocytes. *See* red blood cells
erythropoietin 49
Escherichia coli 98–100, 115
estrogen
age and 38
and breast cancer 9, 47–48
diet and 61–62
functions of 36–37, 61
obesity and 61
regulation of 61–62, *64*
estrogen receptors, chemotherapy drugs blocking 47–48
etoposide 47
eukaryote cells 76–95. *See also* cell(s)
evolution of 76
gene organization in 117
structure of 76–78, *77*
Europe, incidence of cancer in 55–57, *56*, 59
evolution 76
of cancer cells 25–26, 27–28
of eukaryote cells 76
of glycocalyx 94
exons 117

F

family history, and prostate cancer 15
fat
endocrine function of 61–62
in North American diet 59–62
storage in adipocytes 60–61
fatigue, from chemotherapy 48
fatty acids 78, *79*, 80
FDA. *See* Food and Drug Administration
fiber, dietary 62
filter hybridization 104
fluorescent in situ hybridization (FISH) 105
fluorouracil 47
follicle-stimulating hormone (FSH) 61, *64*
food additives, as carcinogens 65
Food and Drug Administration (FDA)
clinical trial applications to 67
interferon approved by 44
photodynamic therapy approved by 52
treatment approval process of 68, 69
FSH. *See* follicle-stimulating hormone
fungal carcinogens, and liver cancer 39, 65

G

gametes
chromosomes in 87–88
meiosis producing 87–90
Gap 0 (G_0) 84
Gap 1 (G_1) *29*, 29–30, 34, 84
Gap 2 (G_2) *29*, 29–30, 34, 84–85
gel, in DNA sequencing 102–103, *104*
gel electrophoresis *97*, 98
Gelsinger, Jesse 110
gender, and bladder cancer 4
genes
cancer caused by 30–34 (*See also* oncogenes)
codons and 92–94
horizontal transfer of 117
human 115–117
content of 116
organization of 117
origins of 116–117
gene swapping 117
gene therapy 50–51, 107–111
clinical trials on 50–51, 110–111
definition of 50
mechanism of 51, *108*, 109–110
natural 117
side effects of 51
vectors used in *108*, 109–110, *110*
genetic abnormality, and cancer cells 22
genetic code 92–94, *93*
genetic mutations
and breast cancer 9
multiple, in cancer cells 25–26
point
definition of 31
in oncogenes 32
in sickle-cell anemia 107–109
in tumor suppressor genes 31–32
genome
eukaryote 76
human 115–117
prokaryote 76
genomic libraries 100

germ cells, lifespan of 20
G4 genome 115
glands
  pituitary, regulation of 61, *63*
  prostate, anatomy of 14–15
  skin 16
Gleditsia sinensis (GSE) 43
gliomas 6
glucose 78, *79*
glycerol 78, *79*
glycocalyx 94–95
  abnormal, in cancer cells 23–24
  composition of 111
  definition of 46, 76
  evolution of 94
  functions of 94–95, 111
  in immune system response 46, 95, 111
  structure of 76, 94, *95*, 111, *112*
  in tissue matching 111
glycolipids
  functions of 94, 111
  production of 76
  structure of *95*, 111, *112*
  in tissue matching 111
  transport of 76–78
glycoproteins
  functions of 94,111
  production of 76
  structure of *95*, 111, *112*
  in tissue matching 46, 111
  transport of 76–78
Golgi complex 76–78, *77*
graft-versus-host disease (GVHD) 46, 54
green tea 43
GSE. *See Gleditsia sinensis*
GTE 43
guanine 80
GVHD. *See* graft-versus-host disease

H

hair loss, from chemotherapy 49
H antigen 111, *114*
haploid cells 90
heart failure, congestive, doxorubicin and 71–72
HeLa cells, immortality of 19
helix, double 82
hemoglobin 45
herbicides, as carcinogens 65
Herceptin 45
hierarchical shotgun sequencing 115–116
HIF-1. *See* hypoxia-inducible factor 1
hippocampus *6*
histones 85
HIV *108*, 109
HLA. *See* human leukocyte antigens
homologous chromosomes (homologs) 88
horizontal transfer, of genes 117
hormone(s). *See also* specific hormones
  age and 38
  regulation of 61–62, *63, 64*
  sex
    diet and 61–62
    and production of cancer 36–37
  steroid, and production of cancer 37
hormone receptors, chemotherapy drugs blocking 47–48
hormone replacement therapy 37
Human Genome Organization (HUGO) 115
human genome project 115–117
human leukocyte antigens (HLA) 113–114
hybridization
  filter 104
  fluorescent in situ 105
hybridomas 45
hydrocephalus 7
hyperacute immune response 114
hypothalamus, in hormone regulation 61, *63, 64*
hypoxia-inducible factor 1 (HIF-1) 43

I

IL-2. *See* interleukin-2
immune system
  in biotherapies 44–45
  effectiveness of, age and 38
  glycocalyx in 46, 95, 111
  hyperacute response in 114
  in transplantation
    bone marrow 46
    tissue matching for 111–115
immunotherapies. *See* biotherapies
incidence 55–66
  age and 37–38
  by continent 55–57, *56*
  definition of *60*
  in developed *vs.* undeveloped countries 57–59, *58*
  diet and 59–62, 66
  environment and 65
  lifestyle and 62–65, 66
  WHO on 55
Indiana University 73
infections
  and bladder cancer 4
  from chemotherapy 49
infectious diseases 107
informed consent, for clinical trials 68

insertional mutagenesis
in gene therapy 51
in oncogenes 32
in situ hybridization, fluorescent 105
interferon 44
interleukin 44
interleukin-2 (IL-2) 44
interphase 84
intervening sequences 117
introns 117
irradiation. *See* radiotherapy

J

Journal of the National Cancer Institute 70
jumping genes 116

K

karyotype
abnormal, in cancer cells 22, *23*
normal *22*
keratin
in basal-cell carcinoma 3
functions of *17*
keratinization *17*
keratosis, actinic 18
kidney cancer, incidence of
by continent *56*
in developed *vs.* undeveloped countries *58, 60*
kinetochores 85, *86*, 87, 88
Krebs cycle 94

L

labeling, of cloned DNA 101
Lacks, Henrietta 19
lambda genome 100, 115
The Lancet (journal) 62
laser therapy 51–52
leptin 61, 62
leukemia(s) 10–12
acute *vs.* chronic 11
bone marrow transplants for 46
definition of 2
diagnosis of 11–12
incidence of
by continent *56*
in developed *vs.* undeveloped countries *58, 60*
Philadelphia chromosome in 22, 35
risk factors for 11
stages of 12
symptoms of 11
types of 11
vector-induced 110–111
leukocyte antigens, human 113–114
leukocytes. *See* white blood cells
Levi, Julia 52
libraries, gene 96, 100–101
lifestyle, and incidence 62–65, 66
linear accelerators 53
liposomes *108*, 109
liver cancer
fungal carcinogens and 39, 65
incidence of
by continent *56*
in developed *vs.* undeveloped countries 57, *58*, 59, *60*
lifestyle and 62
lobes
of breast 8, 9
of lung 13
lobular carcinoma 9
lobules, breast 8
lung
anatomy of *12*, 13
susceptibility to cancer 1
lung cancer 12–14, *13*
asbestos and 14, 39
clinical trials on 72–73
diagnosis of 14
incidence of
by continent *56*
in developed *vs.* undeveloped countries *58, 60*
lifestyle and 62–65
mortality rates for 2, 12
prevalence of 12, 41
risk factors for 14
stages of 14
symptoms of 14
tobacco use and 14, 40–41
lymph nodes 8
lymphocytic leukemia 11
lymphoid cells 11
lymphoma, bone marrow transplants for 46
lysosomes *77*, 78

M

MAbs. *See* monoclonal antibodies
magnetic resonance imaging (MRI)
of brain tumors *7*, 8
of breast cancer 69–70
malignant cancer cells, definition of 36
malignant tumors
definition of 2
spread of (*See* metastasis)
switch from benign to 36
mammography 9, 69–70
MAO. *See* monoamine oxidase
maturation promoting factor (MPF) 85
meiosis 87–90
discovery of 87–88
stages of 88–90, *89*

meiosis I 88–90, *89*
meiosis II 88, 90
melanin
  functions of 16
  in melanoma 3
  production of 16
melanocytes 16, *17*
melanoma 16–18, *18*
  characteristics of 3, 16
  clinical trials on 73–74
Memorial Sloan-Kettering Cancer Center 70
mercaptopurine 47
messenger RNA (mRNA) 92, *93,* 104
metaphase
  of meiosis I *89*
  of mitosis 85, *86*
metaphase checkpoint *29,* 34
metaphase plate 85
metastasis
  angiogenesis in 24, 43
  clinical trials on 74–75
  conditions for 36
  definition of 2
  genes involved in 21–22, 36
  lack of apoptosis and 24
  movement of cancer cells in 24–25, 36
methotrexate 47
microbes 107
microtubules *77,* 78, 85, 87
mitochondria *77,* 78, 94, 115
mitosis (cell division) 85–87
  damage checkpoints in 29–30
  meiosis compared to 88
  stages of 85–87, *86*
mitotic spindle 85
  chemotherapy drugs damaging 47
mixed-function oxidases 40
Mongolia, liver cancer in 59
monoamine oxidase (MAO) 117
monoclonal antibodies (MAbs) 45
monocytes 44
monolayer, cells in 23
monosaccharides 83–84
mortality, by type of cancer 2, *3*
motor proteins *86,* 87
MPF. *See* maturation promoting factor
M phase. *See* mitosis
MRI. *See* magnetic resonance imaging
mRNA. *See* messenger RNA
multicellular organisms, evolution of 28
muscles, cancers of. *See* sarcomas
mutagenesis, insertional
  in gene therapy 51
  in oncogenes 32
mutations. *See* genetic mutations
myc oncogene *32,* 33, 34
myelin 6
myelocytomatosis 3
myelogenous leukemia 11
  Philadelphia chromosome in 22
myeloid cells 10–11

N

NADH dehydrogenase 94
NAG. *See* neodymium aluminum garnet
National Cancer Institute (NCI)
  on chemotherapy 71–72
  on colon cancer 72
  on melanoma 73–74
  on metastasis in spinal cord 74
National Institutes of Health (NIH)
  on carcinogens 38–39
  clinical trial applications to 67
National Research Council, on human genome project 115
natural killer (NK) lymphoctye 44
natural selection, and genetic mutations 26
nausea, from chemotherapy 48
NCI. *See* National Cancer Institute
neodymium aluminum garnet (NAG) laser 52
neoplasm. *See* tumor
nervous system, central 5–6, *6*
neurons 6
neurotransmitters 117
new biology
  coining of term vii
  rise of vii–viii
New England Journal of Medicine 72
NIH. *See* National Institutes of Health
nitrogen, liquid, in cryosurgery 50
NK. *See* natural killer
non-small-cell lung cancer (NSCLC), clinical trials on 72–73
Norris Cotton Cancer Center 72
North America
  cost of treatment in 57
  incidence of cancer in 55–57, *56*
    diet and 59–62
northern blotting 103–104, *106*

NSCLC. *See* non-small-cell lung cancer
nuclear envelope 87
nucleic acids 80–82
nucleolus 76, *77*, 92
nucleotides *79*, 80
  chemotherapy drugs blocking 47
  in nucleic acids 80–82
  structure of *79*, 80
nucleus 76, *77*

O

obesity, and cancer rates 60, 61–62
O blood type 111–113, *114*
occupation, and bladder cancer 4
oligodendrocytes 6
oligodendrogliomas 6
oligo labeling 101
oligosaccharides 83–84
oncogenes 32–34
  deadliness of *33*, 34
  definition of 31
  discovery of xii, 33, 34
  functions of 32, *32*, 34
  naming conventions for 32–34
  production of 32
oncogenesis 27–34
organ transplantation, tissue matching in 111–115
osteoporosis 37
ovarian cancer, incidence of
  by continent *56*
  in developed *vs.* undeveloped countries *58*, *60*
oxidases, mixed-function 40

P

p21 gene, functions of 31, *32*
p53 gene
  functions of 31, *32*
  in gene therapy 51
pain, from chemotherapy 49
pancreatic cancer
  incidence of
    by continent *56*
    in developed *vs.* undeveloped countries *58*, *60*
  mortality rates for 2
PCR. *See* polymerase chain reaction
pemetrexed 73
peptide bonds 80
peroxisomes *77*, 78
pesticides, as carcinogens 65
Phase I clinical trial 67–68
Phase II clinical trial 68
Phase III clinical trial 68
Phase IV clinical trial 69
Philadelphia chromosome (Ph) *21*, 22, 35
phosphate 78, *79*
phospholipids, structure of *81*, 82–83
photodynamic therapy 52
Photofrin. *See* porfimer sodium
phylogeny 76
pipe smoking. *See* tobacco use
pituitary gland, regulation of 61, *63*
plasmids 98–100, *99*, 102
platelets 11, 49
point mutation
  definition of 31, 107
  in oncogenes 32
  in sickle-cell anemia 107–109
  in tumor suppressor genes 31–32
pollution, atmospheric, and lung cancer 14
polyacrylamide gel 98, 102
polymerase chain reaction (PCR) 107
polysaccharides, structure of *81*, 83–84
porfimer sodium 52
postmitotic cells
  evolution of 27–28
  stability of 20
preclinical research 67
primase 90, *91*
primers
  plasmid, in DNA sequencing 102, *102*
  in polymerase chain reactions 107
  random, in labeling cloned DNA 101
progesterone, functions of 36–37
progression, stages of 3–4
prokaryotes 76, 96–98, 117
promoters, gene, mutations in 32
prophase
  of meiosis I *89*
  of mitosis 85, *86*
prostate cancer 14–16
  diagnosis of 15
  diet and 15, 61
  incidence of
    by continent *56*
    in developed *vs.* undeveloped countries 57, *58*, 59, *60*
  mortality rates for 2
  risk factors for 15
  stages of 16
  symptoms of 15
prostate gland, anatomy of 14–15
prostate-specific antigen (PSA) 15
proteins 80, *81*
proto-oncogenes 32–34
  conversion to oncogenes 32
  definition of 31
  naming conventions for 34

protozoans, cancer in 27–28
PSA. *See* prostate-specific antigen
purine *79,* 80
pyrimidine *79,* 80

R

RAC. *See* Recombinant DNA Advisory Committee
race, and bladder cancer 4
radiation
  as carcinogen 39
  cell phone, brain tumors and 6
  ultraviolet, and skin cancer 17
radiotherapy 53
radon, and lung cancer 14
random primer labeling 101
ras oncogene *32,* 32–33
RBC. *See* red blood cells
rb gene, functions of 31, *32*
Recombinant DNA Advisory Committee (RAC) 67–68
recombinant DNA technology. *See* biotechnology
red blood cells (RBC) 10
  in biotherapies 45
  in chemotherapy 49
reproductive cycle
  diet and 61–62
  regulation of 61, *64*
reproductive organs, sex hormones in 36–37
respiratory chain. *See* electron transport chain
restriction enzymes 96–98, 100, 109
retinoblastoma, *rb* gene in 31
retroviruses, in gene therapy 51, *108,* 109
reverse transcriptase 100
Rho gene, in cell motility 36
ribose 78–80, *79*
ribosomal RNA (rRNA) 92
ribosomes *77,* 78, 92
risk factors
  for bladder cancer 4
  for brain tumors 6
  for breast cancer 9
  definition of 4
  for leukemia 11
  for lung cancer 14
  for prostate cancer 15
  for skin cancer 16, 17
Rituxin 45
RNA
  in DNA replication 90, *91*
  functions of 82
  nucleotides in 80, 82
  structure of *81,* 82, *82*
  synthesis of, chemotherapy drugs targeting 47
  in transcription and translation 92
RNA polymerase 92
rRNA. *See* ribosomal RNA

S

Sanger, Fred 101–103, 115
Santillan, Jesica 113, 114
sarcomas
  in chickens xi, xii, 33
  definition of 2
sebum 16
secondary tumors
  in brain 6
  definition of 6
secondhand smoke 14
seminal fluid 14
sensitivity, of breast cancer screening methods 69–70
sequencing, DNA 101–103, *102, 103, 105*
  in human genome project 115–117
sex, and bladder cancer 4
sex hormones
  diet and 61–62
  and production of cancer 36–37
shotgun sequencing, hierarchical 115–116
sickle-cell anemia 107–109
side effects
  of chemotherapy 48–49
  of cryosurgery 50
  of gene therapy 51
  of laser therapy 52
  of photodynamic therapy 52
  of radiotherapy 53
  of stem cell therapy 54
sister chromatids 85, 87
skin
  anatomy of 16
  cells of, susceptibility to cancer 1
skin cancer 16–18
  diagnosis of 18
  incidence of
    by continent *56*
    in developed *vs.* undeveloped countries 57, *58, 60*
  lifestyle and 62
  risk factors for 16, 17
  stages of 18
  symptoms of 17–18
  types of 16
smoking. *See* tobacco use
somatic cells, chromosomes in 87–88
South America, incidence of cancer in 55–57, *56*

Southern, E. M. 104
Southern blotting 103–104
specificity, of breast cancer screening methods 69–70
S phase. *See* DNA synthesis
spinal cord 5
  metastasis in, clinical trials on 74–75
spindle, duplication of 84–85
spindle apparatus *77,* 78
spindle poles 87
squamous cell carcinoma 16–18
squamous cells 16, *17*
src oncogene xii, *32,* 33
stem cells
  functions of 54
  lifespan of 20
stem cell therapy 54
steroid hormones, and production of cancer 37
Stevenson, Robert Louis 19
stomach cancer
  environment and 65
  incidence of
    by continent *56*
    in developed *vs.* undeveloped countries 57, *58,* 59, *60*
The Strange Case of Dr. Jekyll and Mr. Hyde (Stevenson) 19
sugar polymers. *See* polysaccharides
sugars 78–80, *79*
suicide, cellular. *See* apoptosis
sun exposure, and skin cancer 17, 18
SV40 virus 115
Swain, Sandra 71–72
sweat 16
syngeneic bone marrow transplants 46

T

tamoxifen 48
  clinical studies on 70–71
Taxol 47
T cells. *See* T lymphocytes
telomerase 21
  activation of, in cancer cells *33,* 34
telomeres 20–21
telophase
  of meiosis I *89*
  of mitosis 85–87, *86*
testicular cancer, incidence of
  by continent *56*
  in developed *vs.* undeveloped countries *58, 60*
testosterone
  age and 38
  functions of 36–37
testosterone receptors, chemotherapy drugs blocking 48
therapies, cancer 42–54
  angiogenesis blockers as 42–43
  biotherapies 44–45
  bone marrow transplants as 46
  chemotherapy 47–49
  cost of, in North America 57
  cryosurgery 50
  gene 50–51
  laser 51–52
  photodynamic 52
  radiotherapy 53
  stem cell 54
thymine 80
tissue matching 46, 111–115
T lymphocytes (T cells)
  in apoptosis 30
  in biotherapy 44
  functions of 44
tobacco use
  and bladder cancer 4
  carcinogens in 14, 39–41
  in lifestyle 62–65
  and lung cancer 14, 40–41
  secondhand smoke from 14
transcription 92–94, *93*
transformation, of cells 2
translation 92–94, *93,* 117
transplantation
  bone marrow 46
  tissue matching in 46, 111–115
treatment. *See* therapies
trials. *See* clinical trials
TSGs. *See* tumor suppressor genes
tumor(s). *See also* specific types
  benign 2, 36
  cancer cells in 35–36
  malignant 2, 36
  secondary 6
  from single cancer cell 35
tumor suppressor genes (TSGs) 31–32
  definition of 31
  functions of 31–32

U

ultrasonography, in breast cancer diagnosis 9
ultraviolet radiation, and skin cancer 17
undeveloped countries, cancer rates in 57–59, *58*
United Nations, World Health Organization (WHO) established by 55
United States, prostate cancer in 59
University of Bonn 70

University of North Carolina at Chapel Hill 72
uracil 80
urethra 15

V

Varmus, Harold 34
vascular endothelial growth factor (VEGF) 43, 44
vectors
  cloning 109
  in gene therapy *108,* 109–110, *110*
  leukemia induced by 110–111
VEGF. *See* vascular endothelial growth factor
Vinblastine 47
Vincristine 47
viruses
  associated with
    chicken sarcomas xi, xii
  in gene therapy 109
vomiting, from chemotherapy 48

W

WBC. *See* white blood cells
Whilm's carcinoma *23*
white blood cells (WBC) 10–13
  in biotherapies 44, 45
  cancer of. *See* leukemia
  in chemotherapy 49
  types of 10–11
World Health Organization (WHO) 55

X

X-ray therapy. *See* radiotherapy